New Treasures
from the Old

New Treasures from the Old

A Guide to Preaching from the Old Testament

by
J. Alfred Smith, Sr.

Library of Congress Cataloging-in-Publication Data

Smith, J. Alfred (James Alfred)
  New treasures from the old.

  Bibliography: p.
  1. Bible. O.T.—Homiletical use. I. Title.
BS1191.5.S65 1987   221.6   86-30541
ISBN 1-55513-650-8

Dedicated to my former pastorates:

Mt. Washington Baptist Church
Parkville, Missouri;

Second Baptist Church
Huntsville, Missouri;

Second Baptist Church
Columbia, Missouri;

to my present pastorate:

Allen Temple Baptist Church
Oakland, California;

to Mrs. Amy Smith, my mother,
who first taught me the narratives of the Old Testament;

to William Taft Washington
and the legacy of Virginia Hall Washington
for inspiring me to complete the manuscript
when the pressures of the parish presented competing priorities;

and to Dean Laurence Edward Carter, Sr., of Morehouse College
for his refreshing friendship and collegiality
in the training of young preachers.

I am deeply grateful to Ms. Gayle McDonald
for her excellence in typing the manuscript.

Contents

Preface

This book is written at a time when preachers, young and old, apprentices and masters, are in search of a sustaining and profound approach to preaching from the Old Testament.

The pages of this book capture the unique ministry of J. Alfred Smith as seminary professor, Bible scholar, pulpiteer, lecturer, pastor, and president of the Progressive National Baptist Convention and authenticate his ability to provide a guide to Old Testament preaching.

Dr. Smith brings forth from his reservoir of experience and treasures of knowledge, things both new and old that give perspective and depth to the use of the Old Testament in preaching.

The structural principles and approaches used by Dr. Smith encourage faith and give confidence to the preacher often plagued by taboos, uncertainties, and fears in the proclamation of the gems of the Old Testament.

Dr. Smith takes us on a tour of the Old Testament books, explaining their place in history, defining their meaning, describing their purpose, clarifying their mysteries, cataloguing their divine characteristics, and making them live with an applicable and comprehensible meaning.

The reference material is well selected and serves as a guide for research and development for the sincere student of the written inspirations of God.

J. Alfred Smith adds to the field of preaching, especially a dimension of biblical clarity which it very much needs. The following pages will remind us of the wholeness of the word of God and equip us with discerning wisdom, unquestioned authority, and sufficient power to proclaim the great truths of the Old Testament to this age.

Reverend T. L. Willis
Pastor, Pilgrim Hope Baptist Church
Presdient of California Progressive
Baptist Convention and
Assistant to the President of Progressive
National Baptist Convention

Introduction

I was first attracted to the Old Testament as a child by the story-telling of my mother, Mrs. Amy Smith. After explaining to me the story of creation, she introduced me to the stories of the patriarchs and matriarchs of ancient sacred lore. As a growing child my imagination was made vivid by the illustrious preaching of preachers who were specialists in painting scenes from Exodus, Job, and the prophets. I was touched by the music of the Psalms as recorded in the King James Bible. The call narratives of Abraham, Moses, Joshua, Gideon, Samuel, Amos, Isaiah, Jeremiah, and Ezekiel left an indelible impression upon my consciousness. The pathos of Job and the painful agony of Hosea's love for Gomer seemed to resonate with woes of human life heard in my own world. The ethics of Proverbs shaped my religious and moral foundation. The courage of Daniel challenged my commitment to Jesus Christ. The Old Testament theme of liberation became my parallel for the liberation of oppressed persons and nations in the twentieth century.

Upon entering the seminary, an academic hunger for Old Testament study was enriched by my earliest teachers, namely, Dr. Maynard P. Turner, Jr. and Dr. Isadore Keyfitz, who introduced me to the study of biblical Hebrew. In graduate studies I

have become increasingly indebted to Doctors Norman Gottwald and Duane Christensen of whom I am in awe because of
their prodigious mastery of Old Testament scholarship. Dr.
Christensen continues to tutor me in Old Testament studies.

Doctors David T. Shannon, Robert Cate, and Wesley Brown
have aided me far beyond my ability to express in employing the
Old Testament experience of faith in preaching the texts of the
New Testament. Rabbi Samuel Broude and the late Professor
Abraham Heschel have helped me to respect and revere the Old
Testament from a Jewish point of view. Black professor of
theology, James Cone, has encouraged me to view the Old Testament from my experiences as a minority person in America. Professor Elie Wiesel is helping me learn to present Old Testament
characters so that their examples live in our present. Such a feat
is not easy because of the peril of modernizing the Scriptures in
such a way as to rob them of their original historical intention.
Professor Wiesel knows how to do more than just inform us
about the lives of biblical characters. Without ambiguity or
vagueness, he asks the questions of today in the context of the
Old Testament pastor. Preachers E. K. Bailey and Gardner C.
Taylor, along with homileticians James Forbes and Edwina
Hunter, continue to assist and challenge me with their gifts in
nurturing and nourishing. No one of these persons, all to whom I
am deeply indebted, is responsible for any error in this manuscript.

The material in this manuscript was first tested at the National Conference on Preaching which was sponsored in March,
1986 by the Southern Baptist Theological Seminary of Louisville,
Kentucky. President Roy Honeycutt, Dean G. Willis Bennett,
and Professors James Cox and Raymond Bailey opened wide the
doors of opportunity in giving me both the burden of responsibility and the joy of service that resulted in this book. I only
hope that they will not be embarrassed by this work.

The Progressive National Baptist Convention encouraged me
to prepare the manuscript for publication. I would also like to
thank Robert Whitt, Jr., of David C. Cook Publishing for the

assistance he has provided me. I must also give credit to my wife, Mrs. JoAnna Smith, to the office staff of the Allen Temple Baptist Church, to concerned friends, and to the compassionate Allen Temple deacons for their efforts, prayers, and words of encouragement.

J. Alfred Smith, Sr.
Oakland, California
March, 1986

CHAPTER ONE

The Fear of the Old Testament

In preaching circles, one hears clergypersons express fears about preaching from the Old Testament. Many persons express their inhibitions about being unable to preach correctly from texts in the Old Testament. They complain about the intricacies of correctly explaining passages which seem to have no relevance to the challenges of living in a modern age of technology and rapid social change. Some of this fear has been fostered by biblical scholars whose expertise is in sharp contrast with the skills of those parish ministers whose ministry responsibilities prevent them from becoming specialists in Old Testament research. Much Old Testament scholarship is for the continuing dialogue of the academy, whereas the demands of the pulpit require biblical expositions which erudite biblical scholars often look upon with airs of condescension. Often this dilemma promotes an ever-widening gap between pulpits and learned biblical societies.

The cultural world of the Old Testament is alien to the rich cultural pluralism of the modern world. Values, customs, cultural patterns, social stratification, and historical complexities are discussed in literary forms of sagas, epics, narratives, figures of speech, thought forms, and legacies which are antithetical to the world views of the Western world. "Nonscientific" epiphanic and theophanic narration about a burning bush, an ax head floating on the water, or a great fish vomiting up a disobedient prophet may create a credibility gap for modern readers whose minds have been taught to believe only scientific hypotheses and to reject supernaturalism and revelation. The faith of the Enlightenment, an intellectual movement of the eighteenth century, has encouraged the modern world faith in naturalism and natural law. Hence, the modern pulpit has steered away from the strange world of the Old Testament where animals talk and the sun stands still.

The effects of Grecian thinking create a logic contrary to the thought forms of Hebrew language and thought. Very few parish ministers have the discipline or training in biblical Hebrew or the time to acquire and maintain skills in reading the Hebrew Old Testament. Therefore, many pastors are afraid of preaching from biblical texts which they cannot properly translate. Hence, the fear of preaching from the Old Testament persists among persons who religiously forbear from doing violence in interpreting biblical texts.

Ethical codes in the Old Testament seem to be light years in the past from the lofty ethics of Jesus prescribed during the Sermon on the Mount as recounted in the book of Matthew, chapter five. The God of the Old Testament orders the killing of women and children, and even some of the sexual mores of biblical persons seem shocking to modern readers. Can the Old Testament God speak to the modern world in a narrative way? These and other related concerns produce fear in the minds of many who avoid preaching the Old Testament.

Some persons have decided that since the coming of Jesus and the establishing of the New Testament, the only function of the Old Testament is historical—it explains how persons lived until a New Testament ethic was established. Therefore, as this reasoning goes, it is not necessary to preach from the Old Testament because Christ has come. This idea is supported by the anti-Pharisee bias which views the Pharisees as biblical antichrists. The Pharisees are seen as persons who rejected Jesus and embraced Old Testament Law. This bias against the Pharisees has influenced certain persons to not only discard the Old Testament but also to develop an anti-Semitic bias. Unfortunately, some Christians who follow this thinking have become prejudiced against Jews. On the other hand, other Christians have used their understanding of the Old Testament to equate the modern state of Israel with biblical Israel. In an attempt to steer clear of both extremes, not a few Christians ignore the challenge of the Old Testament for preaching.

Some preachers are intimidated by the Old Testament because of their confusion in understanding the Apostle Paul. Since Paul was a Jew, Old Testament law was Paul's possession and pride. Paul was a brilliant student who discovered an enigma with the law. Starting in Exodus 12, during the period of Moses, exhaustive legal prescriptions appear. In Genesis and Exodus 1—11, no legal requirements are set forth. There are narratives about the patriarchs, Abraham, Isaac, Jacob, and Joseph. These early fathers lived prior to the introduction of the law by Moses in Exodus 20, and they walked in peace with God. The literature of Jewish thinkers solved this problem by saying that the patriarchs observed the law given to Moses prior to its promulgation and proclamation. Paul took a different position. The patriarchs, according to Paul, kept the requirements of God without the need of the law. The appearance of Christ provided the opportunity, as in Abraham's time, to achieve God's requirements without the law of Moses. The law of Moses was introduced after the age of the patriarchs and was unnecessary in the new age of Christ. The Mosaic law did function as a tutor to lead persons to Christ. In Romans Paul spoke dialectically about both the deficiency and the utility of the law. (Consider Galatians 3 through 4 and Romans 3:21 through 7:25.)

However, a misunderstanding of Paul can lead one to accept a rejection of the law or what biblical scholars call antinomianism. These persons fail to see that specific legislation, by spelling out prohibitions, could actually prompt persons to do what was forbidden. Persons may not have sinned if the sins had not been mentioned. The rabbis saw the law given to Moses as eternal, whereas Paul saw it as transitory and some of it abrogated in Christ. Moral laws remained valid while ceremonial laws such as food laws, the sacred calendar, animal sacrifices, and other ritualisms were repealed. Many modern proclaimers of the faith who fear the Old Testament law miss this interpretation of Paul.

Perhaps the fear of the Old Testament was born in the Christian church through the thoughts of Marcion who lived during the second century A.D. Marcion believed in a dualistic concept of the universe. "The world is evil because it is materialistic and the heavens are good because they are spiritual," said Marcion. "Because the world is evil, the good God of the New Testament did not create it. The God of the Old Testament made the world. This God was an inferior God of law and justice. He was against the mercy and grace of Christ, the highest emanation of the divine essence." The church excommunicated Marcion in A.D. 144 for his heretical beliefs. "Because of his complete rejection of the Old Testament, Marcion had to omit from his canon much of the New Testament as well."[1]

Friedrich Schleiermacher was almost as bad as Marcion in saying: "The relations of Christianity to Judaism and Heathenism are the same, inasmuch as the transition from either of these to Christianity is a transition to another religion."[2] Adolph Von Harnack in the twentieth century kept alive the nineteenth century fear of the Old Testament of Schleiermacher when he said: "To have cast aside the Old Testament in the second century was an error which the church rightly rejected; to have retained it in the sixteenth century was a fate which the Reformation was not yet able to avoid; but still to keep it after the nineteenth century as a canonical document within Protestantism results from a religious and ecclesiastical paralysis."[3] In 1921 Frederich Delitzsch published *Die Grosse Tauschung* or *The Great Deception*. He argued that anything

1. Foster R. McCurley, Jr., *Proclaiming the Promise*, (Philadelphia: Fortress Press, 1974), p. 8.
2. Friedrich Schleiermacher, *The Christian Faith*, trans. H. R. MacKintosh and J. Stewart, (Edinburgh: T. and T. Clark, 1928), pp. 60-62.
3. Adolph Harnuck, pp. 221-222 from John Bright, *The Authority of the Old Testament*, (Nashville: Abingdon Press, 1967), p. 65.

good in the Old Testament was derivative of the Babylonians. Foster R. McCurley, Jr. tells us that Delitzsch was more destructive than Marcion. Marcion argued as a theologian, but Delitzsch argued as a racist even though he was a respected scholar of Assyriology.[4]

Dr. G. Ernest Wright has shown how some church groups have acted as if the New Testament is the Bible. He said that this error of misusing and disusing the Old Testament deprives the church of the Bible. He saw this tendency most persistent among many American Pentecostal sects.[5]

The mistake of those who fear the Old Testament is rooted in the history of the church. Yet such practice cannot be forgiven. Any serious student of Jesus cannot ignore the love and appreciation Jesus had for the Old Testament. In fact, the only Bible Jesus had was the law, prophets, and writings. Dr. Clyde T. Francisco speaks to the tenor of this argument in explaining:

> Deuteronomy was a favorite book of Jesus, for He quotes from it in each of the three temptations. In other words He did not let its bristling hostility toward Jewish enemies interfere with His appropriation of the themes of love for God and neighbor that form the heart of the book. Nor does He let His consciousness of God's love for all men prevent Him from using language of holy war in describing the battle of the church against its greatest and final enemy, death itself (Matthew 16:18). We too must look for the lasting in the temporal.[6]

Jesus was a Jew. He observed the Jewish religious observances. He frequented the synagogue and the temple. It was Jesus who said: "Think not that I have come to abolish the law and the prophets; I have come not to abolish them but to fulfill them"

---

4. McCurley, op. cit., p. 9.

5. G. Ernest Wright, *God Who Acts: Biblical Theology as Recital*, (Chicago: Alec R. Allenson, Inc., 1952), p. 29.

6. Clyde T. Francisco, *Review and Expositor*, "Preaching from Problem Areas of the Bible," Vol. LXXXII, No. 2, Spring 1975, p. 208.

(Matthew 5:17, RSV). As Jesus began His ministry, we learn:

> He came to Nazareth, where He had been brought up;
> and He went to the synagogue, as His custom was, on the
> Sabbath Day. And He stood up to read; and there was
> given to Him the book of the prophet Isaiah. He opened
> the book and found the place where it was written, 'The
> Spirit of the Lord is upon me because he hath anointed
> me to preach good news to the poor. He has sent me to
> proclaim release to the captives and recovering of sight to
> the blind, to set at liberty those who are oppressed, to pro-
> claim the acceptable year of the Lord.' And He closed the
> book, gave it back to the attendant, and sat down, and
> the eyes of all in the synagogue were fixed on Him. And
> He began to say to them, "Today this scripture has been
> fulfilled in your hearing" (Luke 4:16-20, RSV).

Old Testament scholar Robert Cate has used four powerful arguments of Jesus to substantiate the authority of the Old Testament for Christians based on the lordship of Jesus Christ. Said Dr. Cate:

1. The Old Testament scriptures will stand with an authority until "all is accomplished" (Matthew 5:18).
2. No individual has the right to relax or eliminate the
   authority of the Old Testament (Matthew 5:19).
3. Mere obedience of the law is not sufficient. There was
   probably never any group of people who kept the laws
   of the Old Testament more rigorously than the Pharisees. Yet we are warned that we must be more righteous than they were (Matthew 5:20).
4. To explain what He meant by this last idea, Jesus interpreted a number of the commandments. What He did
   here was to show that there was an underlying principle behind each of the commandments. Rigorous
   obedience to the letter of the law while ignoring the
   deeper principle misses the mark.[7]

Any serious reflection upon the insights shared by Professor Cate as they relate to the authority of the Old Testament viewed through the lens of the lordship of Christ should lead to an abatement of fear of the Old Testament. Indeed, preachers should be afraid to preach from the New Testament without an adequate introduction to the literature and interpretation of the Old Testament.

Preachers who take the time to saturate their minds and soak their imaginations with the exciting world of the Old Testament usually speak with an ineffable beauty. A peerless spokesman from the past who made the Old Testament live in the twentieth century as he preached was the late Dr. Robert G. Lee of the Bellevue Baptist Church of Memphis, Tennessee. Dr. Lee should be studied by students of preaching, since the popular thesis in many seminaries calls for a return to skillful narration in recounting the biblical story. Communication theorists say that in a television age, visual or picturesque speech carries home the message far more effectively than the argumentative and philosophical approach of discursive speech. If these promoters of the new homiletics are true, then the Old Testament has the best possibilities for developing narrative preaching.[8] Before the new literary criticism and new hermeneutics called for a renewal of narrative preaching without fear of the Old Testament, Dr. Robert G. Lee skillfully and scholarly preached life-changing sermons on personalities such as David, Job, Elijah, Elisha, Joel, Jonah, and Amos.

Examples of his illustrious preaching should help to encourage those who are afraid to preach from the Old Testament. Notice

7. Robert Cate, *Old Testament Roots for New Testament Faith*, (Nashville: Broadman Press, 1982), p. 14.

8. Elizabeth Achtemeier, "The Artful Dialogue," *Interpretation*, Vol. XXXV, No. 1, (Richmond, VA: Union Theological Seminary, 1981), pp. 20-29. Old Testament scholar and preacher Elizabeth Achtemeier believes that story preaching has the most promise for preaching. She recognizes Frederick Buechner, Fred Craddock, Edmund Steimle, Morris Niedenthal, Charles Rice, Richard Jensen, and James Sanders as respected authors of books on narrative preaching. Other examples of narrative preaching are found in *Preach On!*, (Nashville: Broadman Press, 1984), J. Alfred Smith, Sr.

how Dr. Lee relates the Psalms to the prophecies of the Messiah. As a Christian preacher, he reads the Old Testament from a Christological perspective. Here Dr. Lee tells about David:

> David, speaking the language of the universal emotions, knowing how to wear the purple, knowing how to grasp the scepter, "the embodiment of his nation's destiny" wrote the Psalms—the Psalms that glow like living coals. But consider how often, whether in "joy hours that make the mountains luminous" or in the imprecatory Psalms, "when the storm spirit puts forth the forest to its lips and blows a trumpet blast of anger," David's verses are filled with prophecies of the Messiah.[9]

Leaving the visual language used in talking about David, the Psalms, and the Messiah, Dr. Lee touches human emotions and answers the question which has made every mind ponder and every heart hope for relief. Using Job and Jesus in contrast, Dr. Lee confronts the Christian audience with an Old Testament text and a Christian affirmation of the resurrection by saying:

> Job, voicing the anguish of generations, reflecting the heart cries of centuries, asking God questions through lips festering with disease, pleading in dense darkness for light, gazing into the future, hearing doubtless amid the whirlwind that stifled the voice of Christ and seeing afar off in centuries a cross tilted, said, his eyes upon Jesus, "I know my redeemer liveth."[10]

Dr. Lee gives a visual picture of the personality, proclamation and purpose of Elijah, and he provides a portrait of the geographical and ecological context in which Elijah was placed in this brief paragraph:

> Sturdy Elijah, tawny with the burning suns of Palestine,

---

9. Robert G. Lee, *Rose of Sharon*, (Grand Rapids, MI: Zondervan, 1974), p. 144.

10. Ibid., p. 114.

stouthearted and thunder voiced with an anger that blazed like the wrath of Achilles, fire and hail and stormy wind authenticity his divine mission, a union of the terrible with the gentle, calling an apostate nation back to God.[11]

Old Testament history is utilized and a spiritual incarnation is manifested with accompanying expressions of God's powers along with the preacher's own Christological vision as Dr. Lee asks the hearers to:

Consider Elisha, wrapped in an aura of profoundest spiritual truth, the honored mouthpiece of God at the court of six kings, miracles without number credited to him, anticipating more than Elijah the spirit of Jesus Christ.[12]

The prophetic dimensions of the Old Testament that point to historical New Testament realities are areas of preaching which Christian preachers should not overlook. In a short utterance on Joel, Dr. Lee blends God's judgment, repentance, prayer, and the prophecy of the day of Pentecost into a harmonious chord of gospel that mingles the emotions of sadness, gladness, and expectancy into a melody for listening and reflecting. Such use of the Old Testament comes from not fearing the Old Testament but from being challenged by it. This preacher accepts the challenge and calls the hearers to accept the challenge with the imperative:

"Think of Joel—at a time when locusts cursed the earth, he asked people to rend their hearts and not their garments—asked for a day of national humiliation and prayer —foresaw God's Spirit being poured upon all flesh."[13]

You, too, can develop your story after studying this master or

11. Ibid., p. 114.
12. Ibid., pp. 114-115.
13. Ibid., p. 115.

other masters who are adept at making the Old Testament speak with freshness and power.

The major centers of power and commerce, with sensate life styles and insatiable appetites for violence and exploitation are as ripe for prophetic preaching from the Old Testament as cities were when Dr. Lee first preached:

> Remember Jonah. Behind the curtain of his fearless preaching, old Nineveh, once gay and giddy, strutting and sinful, no longer shoots defiant fists, but bent humble knees.[14]

The universality of God's judgment and the basis for its housing in the concept of ethical monotheism is needed today in view of the secularizing of religion and the equating of religion with nationalism on the part of some who are leaders of the familiarly called moral majority. Cultural Christianity that automatically justifies whatever western nations do and the coaptation of the church by the values of consumerism and militarism need the corrective preaching that comes when persons heed Dr. Lee's admonition to:

> Give thought to Amos, the soul of fury. He impeached civilizations, summoned the nations to judgment. At a time when the outside of the cup was polished, the inside tarnished and foul, "his eye and lips threw flame as he condemned Damascus for cruelty, Gaza for torturing slaves, Tyre for voluptuousness, Edom for savage lust, Moab for scarlet vice, and Israel for using the temple of idolatry for a winding sheet around Jehovah's altars.[15]

There is an eternal or timeless quality about the preaching of the Old Testament. Race, nationality, geography, or denomination seem to have very little to do with authentic explication and exposition of sacred Scripture. If the preachers are fearless in proclamation, and if they are not afraid of the Old Testament, power-

14. Ibid., p. 115.
15. Ibid., p. 115.

ful similiarities emerge, as the reader will observe, in comparing the Old Testament preaching of Dr. Robert G. Lee with Dr. Allan Boesak, a black South African theologian active in the movement against apartheid. Dr. Lee was a white Southern Baptist preacher. But Dr. Boesak is a young ordained minister of the Dutch Reformed Mission Church. He undertook his theological studies at the Theological Academy of Kampen in the Netherlands. Dr. Boesak's comments are based on the words of 2 Chronicles 16:12.

> In the thirty-ninth year of his reign Asa was diseased in his feet, and his disease became severe; yet even in his disease he did not seek the Lord, but sought help from the physicians (2 Chronicles 16:12).

Dr. Boesak uses as his sermon topic "Whence Comes Our Help?" He reminds the hearers that doctors and medicine are not attacked in the text. The intent of the passage is to show that Asa became ill because he did not trust God. In the Old Testament, sickness was seen as an opportunity for reflection, meditation, and communion with God. Asa, however, forgot Psalm 103:3 which spoke of God as He "who heals all your diseases." So here was Asa, estranged from God, when his people were diseased in politics, and he was diseased physically and spiritually. This sad illness was fatal. A sickly king over the kingdom of Judah was unable to defend his kingdom for his brother, Baasha, King of Israel.

Notice the application that Dr. Boesak makes. It could easily have been the utterances of Dr. Lee:

> Asa is not dead. He lives on in our midst. The sins of Asa are not foreign to us. Christians behave today exactly as did Asa. They behave foolishly. We place our trust in our own efficacy, in our own capabilities. We believe that our organizational skill, our money, and our intellectual prowess are alone sufficient.[16]

---

16. Allan Boesak, *The Finger of God: Sermons on Faith and Socio-Political Responsibility*, translated from the Afrikaans by Peter Randall, (New York: Mary Knoll, Orbis Books, 1979), pp. 23-24.

With the affinity for the prophets which the reader saw in Dr. Robert G. Lee, Dr. Allan Boesak speaks with the courage of Amos, the invective of John the Baptist, and the passionate pleading of Hosea in pronouncing:

> How sick our country is! What we see on the outside —apartheid, humiliation, hatred, suspicion, the destruction of families, migrant labor—are merely the stinking boils on the surface, symptoms of all that is devouring us internally. Oppression, anxiety, suspicion, and distrust wreck our chances for authentic reconciliation. And in the meanwhile we remain mute before the misery and we argue in the press about whether women should wear hats in church! Even in his disease Asa did not seek the Lord. . . . May God forgive us! And He will.[17]

There are treasures in the Old Testament waiting to be mined. Persons like Lee and Boesak have shown that the treasures can be profitably mined through skillful use of theological and hermeneutical methodology. An understanding of the approaches to the study of the Old Testament will help to minimize the fear some preachers have experienced in using Old Testament texts for preaching. Attention will now be given to defining the major approaches that scholars have used in Old Testament studies.

17. Ibid., pp. 23-24.

CHAPTER TWO

Approaches to the Study of the Old Testament

There are authorities who begin their writings with Abraham, Isaac, and Jacob. Some start with Moses and the Exodus events. Not a few scholars start with the settlement in the land of Canaan while others start with the rise of the Hebrew monarchy under King Saul. The theological assumptions of the scholars determine where they begin their writings. Theologians of the Old Testament often start with a development of the idea of God in the thinking of the Hebrew people.

Dr. Robert Cate suggests that the easiest way to start is with an *historical approach*. He lists the following historical periods:

1. *The Patriarchal Period*
   2000 to 1700 B.C.
2. *The Period of the Sojourn in Egypt*
   1700 to 1300 B.C.
3. *The Period of the Exodus and the Wilderness*
   1280 to 1240 B.C.
4. *The Period of the Conquest and the Settlement*
   1240 to 1020 B.C.
5. *The Period of the United Monarchy*
   1020 to 931 B.C.

6. *The Period of Israel and Judah as Separate Kingdoms*
   931 to 721 B.C.
7. *Judah's Period Alone*
   721 to 586 B.C.
8. *The Period of Babylonian Exile*
   586 to 539 B.C.
9. *The Persian Period*
   539 to 333 B.C.
10. *The Greek Period*
    333 to 168 B.C.[18]

In beginning either a study or a series of sermons from the Old Testament, preachers will find it easier to preach from a particular period or to relate the text to a specific historical age rather than preaching from the Old Testament without helpful context which can encourage interest and understanding.

Professor Walter C. Kaiser, Jr., of Trinity Evangelical Divinity School of Deerfield, Illinois, uses *a theological approach* rather than an historical one. Professor Kaiser notes that theologians use four basic approaches. Recognizing these four basic theological approaches will enable beginning students to understand the authors who are sharing the insights they have gleaned from Old Testament research. Kaiser defines them as:

1. *The structural type,* which borrows from systematic theology, sociology, or selected theological principles and traces its relationship to secondary concepts. Scholars in this camp are Eichrodt, Vriezen, and Vandmschoot.
2. *The diachronic type* sets forth the theology of the successive time period and stratifications of Israelite history. Unfortunately the emphasis falls on the successive traditions of the religious community's faith and experience. The leading scholar of this type is Von Rad.

18. Robert Cate, *Old Testament Roots for Our Faith* (Nashville: Broadman Press, 1982), pp. 19-20.

3. *The lexicographic type* limits its scope of investigation to a group of biblical men and their special theological vocabulary, for example, the sages', the Elohist, the Priestly, and the Yahwist vocabulary. Recognized scholars of this type are Gerhard Kittel and G. W. Bromiley of the *Theological Dictionary of the New Testament* and Peter F. Ellis. The Yahwist: *The Bible's First Theologian*, (Notre Dame: Fides Publishers, 1968).

4. *The biblical themes type* presses its search beyond the vocabulary of the single key term to encompass whole constellations of words around a key theme. Persons who are well-known for using this type are John Bright, who is famous for his work on the Kingdom of God, and Paul and Elizabeth Achtemeier, who gave to us the work on *The Old Testament Roots of Our Faith*.[19]

Professor J. N. Schofield, lecturer in Hebrew and Old Testament Studies at the University of Cambridge, stressed God in his works under the classifications of "The God Who Acts," "The God Who Speaks," "God's Kinship with Man," and "The Glory of God." This is an easy approach for a preacher just beginning to preach from Old Testament texts. Lay persons and specialists will enjoy the work by Professor John L. McKenzie. His work, *A Theology of the Old Testament*, skillfully treats the topics of cult, revelation, history, nature, wisdom, political and social institutions, and the future of Israel. Seminal preaching ideas and sermon material that have enriched my preaching have come from Professor Walter Brueggeman's books, *The Land*, and *Prophetic Imagination*. Brueggeman writes in the heritage of Von Rad as an historian of the traditions of Israel's faith while using all of the skills of those who are of the lexicographic type of scholarship. In fact, no one type can be utilized as the only approach for discovering the vitality the Old Testament has in store for preaching. Pro-

19. Walter C. Kaiser, Jr., *Toward an Old Testament Theology*, (Grand Rapids, MI: Zondervan, 1978), pp. 9-10.

fessor Ralph W. Klein gives an excellent theological interpretation of Israel in exile. Professor George A. E. Knight ignores the documentary hypothesis and shares fresh insights on Exodus in his *Theology as Narration*. Professor Donald E. Gowan uses major genres of literature such as history, saga, short story, law, wisdom, and prophecy and uses traditional history in his *Reclaiming the Old Testament for the Christian Pulpit*. Dr. James Sanders speaks of using prophetic hermeneutics in order to read a text so as to see the full humanity of the persons spoken of in the text. He moves away from a challenging hermeneutic of prophetic dimensions to a constitutive or supporting hermeneutic for pastoral preaching in his work *God Has a Story Too*. Professor Sanders reminds pastors that Old Testament approaches to preaching can stress singularly or together, depending upon sermon text and context, the freedom of God and the grace of God.

The approaches to the study of the Old Testament cannot be fully discussed in one manuscript. Nevertheless, those who are serious about the challenge of the Old Testament will not allow sloth to kill the quest to understand the volumes of insight that respectable scholars are providing, not only for scholarly debate, but also for tools in the weekly work of sermon preparation and continuing education.

For this writer, the clearest explanation of scholarly debate for those whose major task is to preach from the Old Testament comes from the writings of Professor Marvin E. Tate of Southern Baptist Theological Seminary in Louisville, Kentucky. This explanation is lucidly expressed in an article entitled *Old Testament Theology: The Current Situation*. Dr. Tate brings the works of the Old Testament into three categories rather than the four expressed by Professor Walter Kaiser, Jr. The three categories of Tate are: (1) the systematic synthetic approach, (2) the tradition-history approach, and (3) the eclectic approach.[20]

---

20. Marvin E. Tate, "Old Testament Theology: The Current Situation," *Review and Expositor*, Vol. LXXIV, No. 3, Summer 1977, Louisville, KY, pp. 288-295.

The systematic method refers to that approach which utilizes the traditional themes such as God, man, salvation, and eschatology. Some well-known persons who have used this approach have been Otto Baab, Paul Heinisch, Paul Van Imschoot, and J. Barton Payne. These themes have had practical preaching value for centuries in the history of the church.

The "term synthetic" approach has worked to bring separate thematic elements into integrated wholes. The leading writer of this method has been Walter Eichrodt. The historical principle and the systematic principle operate side by side to compose a complementary rule in Eichrodt's works. He uses a three-part outline consisting of God and the People, God and the Word, and God and the World in his attempt to understand the Old Testament in its structural unity.

Professor Edmond Jacob also uses a synthetic approach. Jacob used two themes: the presence of God and the action of God. The purpose of God's action was said to maintain and create life through the Spirit and the Word. Jacob saw God's action in kings, prophets, priests, wise men, places, cult, and law. He also wrote about sin, redemption, death, future life, eschatology, and Messianic Kingdom.

Gerhard Von Rad, whom Kaiser classified as a user of the diachronic method, is associated with the tradition-history method. Von Rad states that the method of the Old Testament is that of retelling and not that of producing a synthesis of the theological message of the Old Testament. Von Rad is concerned with how Israel preserved and passed on its faith through the creedal statements that are found in Scripture. Von Rad called the faith of Israel salvation history or *heilsgeschichte*. The history to which Von Rad pointed is not the critical historiography of the scholars but the faith content which Israel believed and arranged in her creedal compositions such as Deuteronomy 6:20-24, 26:5b-9, and Joshua 24:2b-13.

Von Rad's work has been the topic of controversy. Some scholars have disagreed with Von Rad's argument that Old Testament theology cannot have a center point of focus. Walter

Eichrodt counters that the true focal point was the covenant which revealed a transcendent God who chose Israel to be a community who would choose to be responsive to the will of God. Von Rad's critics urge that his center was the belief in God's self-revelation in history as expressed in the history of the Deuteronomistic tradition. Professor George Fohrer argues for a dual focal point that embraces the lordship of God and the communion between God and persons. Professor C. Vriezen states that the one focal point of all history was communion between God and Israel. Professor Rudolf Smend pleads a dual focal point which dealt with Yahweh, the God of Israel and Israel, the people of God. Professor Gerhard Hasel speaks of a multi-focal approach where God as the center brought together the numerous Old Testament testimonies from beginning to end, and Professor W. Zimmerli quotes Exodus 20:2 and Deuteronomy 6:5 which emphasize "I am Yahweh, your God" as the foundation point of Old Testament focus.

Professor Gerhard Von Rad has helped Old Testament students to appreciate not only the theology of the prophets but also wisdom theology. As far as scholarly writings are concerned, wisdom literature has been a neglected area of investigation. Professor Walter Zimmerli has related wisdom literature to creation theology. Von Rad has contributed much toward stimulating discussion among scholars about the tradition-history approach.

Professor John L. McKenzie argues for the eclectic method. Dr. McKenzie stresses his view that the Bible is irrelevant to systematic theology. He does not see a rational system in the Old Testament. McKenzie promotes the treatment of God as a personal reality who must be related to those topics in the Scripture which encounter the questions asked by the world and the church in each of the changing historical contexts of history. Professor McKenzie has astonished Old Testament scholars by his refusal to accept a justification for using the Old Testament by many Christians. He also rejects the Messianic element in the Old Testament. Professor McKenzie's thesis:

The task of Old Testament theology for the Christian

could not be conceived simply as the total description of that being whom Jesus called his father. The Christian Old Testament theologian ought to do at least this; perhaps it is all he can do. This, it will be observed, leaves almost no room for prediction, foreshadowing, allegory, or typology; and these techniques will not be employed in this work.[21]

Nevertheless, those of us who disagree with Professor McKenzie on this point can find agreement with him on his view that the Old Testament provides a study of the reality of God. The theories of scholars can stimulate preachers to clarify their personal beliefs and strengthen them for pulpit proclamation. It is this same certitude that has enabled Dr. Gardner C. Taylor, the "dean of preachers," to utter:

> Christ is that scarlet thread behind which our souls are safe when the enemy comes and the storm of battle rages. Christ is that scarlet thread behind which we who trust Him may have the blessed assurance that it is well with our souls. Christ is that scarlet thread, the sinners' perfect plea, the seekers' end of the search, the saints' everlasting rest, a hiding place when the storms are raging. I speak of Christ as the scarlet thread of safety and security when enemies beseige our souls, when friends fail us and forsake us, as bread in a starving land and rivers of water in a dry and barren place. Christ, our Passover, Christ, the first fruits of them that sleep, Christ, the end of the law and the first of many brethren. Mary's baby and older than Abraham. Christ, our great High Priest. Christ, our Scarlet Thread.[22]

Using the method of typology, Dr. Taylor built his message upon Joshua 2:18-19: "Behold, when we come into the land, thou shalt bind this line of scarlet thread in the window which thou

21. John L. McKenzie, A Theology of the Old Testament, (Garden City, NY: Image Books, 1976), p. 31.
22. Gardner C. Taylor, The Scarlet Thread, (Elgin, IL: Progressive Baptist Publishing House, 1981), p. 19.

didst let us down by: and thou shalt bring thy father, and thy mother, and thy brethren, and all thy father's household, home unto thee . . . and whosoever shall be with thee in the house, his blood shall be on our head, if any hand be upon him."

The use of typology which Professor McKenzie rejects presupposes that even though differences exist between the Old Testament and the New Testament, there is a fundamental parallel in that the same God who revealed Himself in the salvation of the covenant people of Israel is the same God who has spoken to us in Jesus Christ. Typology is a unifying thread between both the Old and New covenants. While Gardner C. Taylor used typology to express similarity, the Apostle Paul in Romans 5 used typology to express contrast between Adam and Jesus Christ, the second Adam. Nevertheless, the common note of both preachers in the use of typology was a satisfying coherence which upholds a strong concept of the unity of Old and New Testament Scriptures.

Other approaches to the Old Testament will allow parish ministers to preach from the Old Testament from: (1) the perspective of the Old Testament as faith; (2) the prose of the Old Testament as law and a way of wisdom for living; (3) the old Testament as poetry for praise or worship of the only true and living God; (4) the Old Testament as promulgation of the history of salvation; (5) the Old Testament as a portrait (partially in promise) of Christ; and (6) the Old Testament as the presentation of the Scripture or canon. Potential for preaching from the Old Testament presents pregnant possibilities more than adequate for challenging persons who wear the prophetic mantle of preaching.

Those who preach are deeply indebted to Old Testament scholars who have refined and defined again and again approaches for understanding and applying Old Testament Scriptures to the needs of the modern world. Preachers will need to encounter the powerful presence of the living God in the critical approach to the Scriptures. Unless this can be done, the hard work of analytical and reflective study of the Scriptures will be an exercise in futility. Professor Duane Christensen of the American Baptist Seminary of the West and the Graduate Theological Union in Berkeley,

California urges preachers to utilize serious academic methodology while encouraging a biblical theology of God's presence which comes as a result of prayerful reflection upon the texts in the Old Testament canon. In a class for lay persons and clergy taught in the fall of 1985 at Allen Temple Baptist Church in Oakland, California, Professor Christensen encouraged the class to seriously examine *The Elusive Presence* by Union Theological Seminary of New York's emeritus professor, Dr. Samuel Terrien. It is Dr. Terrien's belief that the reality of God's presence is the heart of biblical theology. Said Dr. Terrien, "The reality of divine presence proved to be the constant element of distinctiveness throughout the centuries of biblical times. It is this reality which produced the power of a canonical Scripture, and it is this reality which may renew this power in contemporary Christianity.[23] Very few persons who preach from week to week would oppose this argument. In fact, Professor Terrien brings a welcome word of challenge and comfort that can heal any cleavage between a scientific approach and a spiritual approach to the study of the sacred Scriptures.

Attention has been given to a discussion of the fear of preaching from the Old Testament, and the overcoming of that fear through the effective use of time-tested, scholarly approaches to utilizing the Old Testament. It is now logical to discuss in the forthcoming chapter some of the homiletical themes of the Old Testament. These themes are related to the discussion of scholarly approaches to the Old Testament.

23. Samuel Terrien, *The Elusive Presence: The Heart of Biblical Theology*, (San Francisco: Harper and Row, 1983), p. 43.

CHAPTER THREE

Selected Theological Themes for Preaching the Old Testament

Whereas the Egyptians introduced the doctrine of monotheism, the Hebrew people not only embraced this idea of one God, but also for the very first time in recorded history they taught the idea of ethical monotheism. That one God is holy, moral, and ethical. Polytheism is the belief in many gods. Henotheism advocates the selection of one god from the pantheon to worship and obey. But ethical monotheism insists on believing in Yahweh, the one and only supernatural being who creates, controls, and sustains creation out of love for the goodness of creation. This God is not capricious, nor does this God act from immoral motivation. A careful reading of Genesis 1 reveals this idea. Genesis 2 and 3 uphold the morality or holiness with which Yahweh relates to creatures and the creation as the Creator.

In Exodus 15:11 the song of Moses asks: "Who is like thee, O Lord, among the Gods? Who is like thee, majestic in holiness, terrible in glorious deeds, doing wonders?" In Isaiah 43:3 the holiness of God emerges: "For I am the Lord, your God, the Holy One of Israel, your Saviour." The ancient world saw no relationship between religion and morality. T. H. Robinson advises us that in the ancient world there was hardly a vice or crime which could not be committed, not merely with connivance, but with the sanction and even the direct authority of one of the numerous deities. So complete was the divorce between religion and morality that not a few of the great souls of the ancient world discarded the gods altogether. To them religion and righteousness were incompatible.[24]

The Decalogue was given in Exodus 20:1-17 and Deuteronomy 5:6-21. Both are ethical in content. Exodus 34:10-26 is concerned with ritual. In Deuteronomy 4:13 and 10:4 it is called the Ten Commandments and in Exodus 25:16 it is called the Testimony. Leviticus 17—26 is called the Holiness Code. Leviticus 19 has been given greater honor than the Decalogue. The basis for Hebrew morality is Leviticus 19:26: "You shall be holy to me; for I the Lord am holy, and have separated you from the peoples, that you should be mine."

In Exodus 19:6 the Hebrew people are told by God: "You shall be to me a kingdom of priests and a holy nation. . . ." A holy God selects holy people. This idea logically leads to the theme of covenant. (The preacher should remind the people, who on a daily basis also face human-made law, that God's covenant is to be distinguished from a contract. Unlike a contract, the covenant was not "negotiated" between God and the people. God presented the covenant He established *for* the people *to* the people simply to be accepted and embraced, but not to be "renegotiated" or redefined.)

God is a covenant-making, covenant-keeping, and covenant-revealing God. In each instance where a covenant was made between God and the people, the initiation was from God. The purpose for a covenant was to provide a binding relationship or commitment between God and the people. The covenant also expressed God's intentionality and love for the people with whom He made the covenant.

The covenant-making God established His covenant with

24. T. H. Robinson, *Prophecy and the Prophets*, (London: Duckworth, 1923), p. 5.

Noah in Genesis 6:18, with Abraham in Genesis 15:18 and 17:2, with David in 2 Samuel 23:5, with Israel and Judah in Jeremiah 31:31-34, and He made an everlasting covenant in Isaiah 55:3 and 61:8.

God keeps His covenant according to Deuteronomy 7:9, 2 Chronicles 6:14, and Psalm 111:5, 9. In Psalm 25:14 and Deuteronomy 1:31 the faithfulness and reliability of God's promises are evidenced by the terms revealing the nature of the covenant. Certain of God's covenants have the promises of blessings or curses confirmed with an oath which makes them irrevocable. See Genesis 26:23, 33, Jeremiah 11:5, and Zechariah 8:17. The breaking of the oath often resulted in the infliction of a curse such as in Nehemiah 5:12, 10:29, Ezekiel 16:59, Daniel 9:11, and Numbers 5:19-25.

For the value of preaching in a Christian context, the seed of David finds its fulfillment in Jesus Christ. Jesus was David's Lord and root as to His divinity but was David's son and offspring as to His humanity. The writer to the Hebrews applied the father-son clause of the Davidic Covenant to Jesus Christ. Compare 2 Samuel 7:11-16 and 1 Chronicles 17:11-15 with Hebrews 1:5.

Under the Abrahamic Covenant, God chose the nation of Israel, and from the nation, He chose a tribe which was Judah. Under the Davidic Covenant He chose a family. This family was the family of Jesse of which David was a member. Read Genesis 17:6, 16, 49:8-12, and Psalms 78:67-72 and 89:3, 4. This promise finds its fulfillment in the unbroken dynasty of Davidic kings from Solomon to Zedekiah in the promised land. The dynasty of David is as follows:

1. Solomon—1 Kings 1-11.
2. Rehoboam—1 Kings 12—14.
3. Abijam—1 Kings 15:1-18; 2 Chronicles 12:1-22.
4. Asa—1 Kings 15:11; 2 Chronicles 14—16.
5. Jehoshaphat—1 Kings 15:24; 2 Chronicles 17—20.
6. Jehoram—1 Kings 22:50; 2 Kings 8:16-24;
   2 Chronicles 21.

7. Ahaziah—2 Kings 11:4-21; 2 Chronicles 22:1-9.
8. Joash—2 Kings 11:4-21; 2 Chronicles 24; 25.
9. Amaziah—2 Kings 12:21; 14:1-20; 2 Chronicles 24; 25.
10. Uzziah—2 Kings 14; 15; 2 Chronicles 26.
11. Jotham—2 Kings 15:32-38; 2 Chronicles 27.
12. Ahaz—2 Kings 15:38; 16:1, 2; 2 Chronicles 28.
13. Hezekiah—2 Kings 18; 20; 2 Chronicles 28—32.
14. Manasseh—2 Kings 21:1-18; 2 Chronicles 33.
15. Amon—2 Kings 21; 2 Chronicles 33:20-25.
16. Josiah—2 Kings 22; 23; 2 Chronicles 34; 35.
17. Jehoahaz—2 Kings 23:31-34; 2 Chronicles 36:1-4.
18. Jehoiakim—2 Kings 23:34-37; 24:1-6; 2 Chronicles 36:5-8.
19. Jehoiachin—2 Kings 24:6-17; 2 Chronicles 36:9-10.
20. Zedekiah—2 Kings 24:17-20; 25; 2 Chronicles 36:11-21.

Zedekiah was the last Davidic king to reign over the house of Judah in the land of Canaan. His reign ended with the destruction of Jerusalem and the temple, the captivity of Judah to Babylon and the death of the royal sons. This is the end of the biblical record of the national Davidic throne. This reality seems to contradict the promise God had made to David that his seed, throne, and kingdom would endure as the sun and the moon remained. Read Psalms 89:3, 4, 29-39, 132:11-12, and Jeremiah 33:17-26.

The prophet Ezekiel, in anticipating the fall of Zedekiah, left a flicker of hope in saying, "A ruin, ruin, ruin I will make of it; there shall not be even a trace of it until he comes whose right it is and to him will I give it" (Ezekiel 21:27). Three theories have struggled with the historical discontinuity of the Davidic throne. The scholars who embrace anyone of these theories are not satisfied with the explanation given by Ezekiel.

The first theory says that the Davidic Covenant was a revocable covenant as evidenced by the conditions laid down in the wording of the covenant. The failure of the majority of the kings to keep the terms of the covenant was the reason God revoked and annulled the covenant. Read 2 Samuel 7:14, 15, Psalms

89:29-32, and 132:11-12. Those who reject this argument say that it is impossible for God to annul a covenant that has been confirmed with an oath.

The second theory says that natural fulfillment of a dynastic succession was not necessary after the time of Zedekiah. This is so because of the spiritual fulfillment that came 600 years later in Jesus Christ. The weakness of this argument is that such a reality would be a breach of the promise that was made when the covenant was established. Can a throne be vacant for 600 years when it was set forth in a covenant that a vacancy would never occur?

The third theory wages that the house of Judah was the natural throne of David but later became a part of the British Isles through the efforts of Jeremiah. It was Jeremiah who brought a daughter of King Zedekiah of the Judah-Pharez-Davidic line to be married to a prince of the Judah-Zarah line. Thus, the lineage of the kings of Ireland, Scotland, and England was the ongoing fulfillment of the Davidic covenant. The issue of merging secular history with religious or biblical history is the crux of the problem.

In Luke 1:32, the note of fulfillment of the Davidic Covenant is clearly played:

> He will be great, and will be called the Son of the Most High, and the Lord God will give to him the throne of his father David: and he will reign over the house of Jacob forever; and of his kingdom there will be no end.

Early Christian preaching kept emphasizing the same note that was played by Luke, that Jesus Christ is the fulfillment of the Davidic Covenant. They taught that (1) the Davidic Covenant was not a revocable covenant and (2) the God of ethical monotheism is a covenant-making, covenant-keeping, and covenant-revealing God. Logically, the next theme of prominence in the Old Testament is Israel, the people of God.

In Genesis 32:28 the name Israel appears for the first time. An angel said to Jacob, "Your name shall no more be called Jacob, but Israel, for you have striven with God and with men, and have prevailed." An inscription produced by Pharaoh Merneptah carries the name "Israel stele." It records the names of the population conquered in his military campaigns. Here Israel appears as a people who are still nomads or in a preorganized national status. This stele has been dated around 1230 B.C., doubtless but a short time after the exodus from Egypt, and indicates that the name Israel as a designation of the Hebrews was already known in the 13th century.

Israel was brought into a union of tribal people not for any political reason or by any nationalistic purpose. Their bond was a common worship of and allegiance to Yahweh, the God of the patriarchs, the God who had promised the land to the seed of Abraham and Jacob, and who had delivered His people from their bondage in Egypt, who had led them in the wilderness and was now giving them the promised land.

In Judges 5:2, 7-11, the song of Deborah reveals how several tribes came together because of their awareness of belonging to the same cultic community.

> Then sang Deborah and Barak, the son of Abin'o-am, on that day: That the leaders took the lead in Israel, that the people offered themselves willingly, bless the Lord!
>
> The peasantry ceased in Israel, they ceased until you arose, Deborah, arose as a mother in Israel. When new gods were chosen, then war was in the gates. Was shield or spear to be seen among forty thousand in Israel? My heart goes out to the commanders of Israel who offered themselves willingly among the people. Bless the Lord. Tell of it you who ride on tawny asses, you who sit on rich carpets and you who walk by the way. To the sound of musicians at the watering places, there they repeat the triumphs of the Lord, the triumphs of his peasantry in Israel (Judges 5:2, 7-11, RSV).

A common credo by the tribes in the presence of Joshua at Shechem is discovered in Joshua 24. This faith in Yahweh bound people to Yahweh and to each other. This is why the people referred to themselves as people of Israel, children of Israel, and house of Israel.

Once the people acquired a political government and secured a king, the term "Israel" underwent a change that added geographical and nationalistic meanings. The southern tribes of Judah and Simeon remained somewhat aloof from the confederation, and it became impossible at times to rally all of the tribes into a unified body to fight for common survival. Saul, the first king, did not succeed in creating national unity according to 1 Samuel 11:8. According to 2 Samuel 2:1-4, David, at first, was king only of Hebron, while Ishbosheth was king of Israel. (See verses 8-11.) Some seven and a half years later David became king of all Israel and Judah. (See 2 Samuel 5:5.)

In *The Hebrew Bible: A Socio-Literary Introduction*, Professor Norman K. Gottwald places emphasis upon the common oppression of those persons who left Egypt en route to the promised land with Moses. Dr. Gottwald argues that:

> Once the Moses group entered Canaan and joined with other peoples to form the confederation of Israel, the earlier distinguishing traits of the group were merged with the cultural norms and historical experiences pooled by the whole body of Israel and the group's distinctive socio-religious organization was restructured in the design of a vastly expanded and elaborated system of tribes in mutual aid.[25]

Having been both a student and pastor of Dr. Gottwald, this author is in awe of the prodigious ability and voluminous knowledge which his writings and lectures reveal. His conclusions have encouraged ongoing debate and discussion such as:

1. Did the sociology of oppression bring the oppressed into a confederation?
2. Did Yahweh bring them into this union as the God who liberates the oppressed?
3. Did pragmatism that creates holy coalitions among di-

25. Norman K. Gottwald, *The Hebrew Bible: A Socio-Literary Introduction*, (Philadelphia: Fortress Press, 1985), p. 224.

verse, unholy people create unity for the sole motive of survival?

Dr. Gottwald may not offer conclusive answers in the same manner as traditional biblical theologians. But he will inspire preachers to do their own hard thinking before preaching a seemingly easy and elementary sermon on Old Testament biblical texts. The sociological approach of Gottwald should assist preachers in identifying causal factors in the split between the northern and southern regions of the Hebrew nation after the death of King Solomon.

At the time of the complete break, Israel became the designation of the northern kingdom and Judah was the name for the southern kingdom under the Davidic dynasty. Geographically, Israel was the mountainous area of Ephraim. (See Joshua 11:16-21.) The kings of Israel, of whom the first was Jeroboam, continued to reign in the northern kingdom for about two hundred years until the Assyrians invaded the land, destroyed the capital Samaria, and put an end to the monarchy in Israel (722-721 B.C.).

Instead of using the word "Judah" after the demise of the northern kingdom, the word "Israel" was used to describe the southern kingdom as the genuine remnant of the people of God maintained by the Davidic house. (See Isaiah 5:7, Micah 3:1, Jeremiah 2:4, 10:1, and Isaiah 41:14.)

After the fall of Jerusalem in 586 B.C., the Babylonian exile, and the period of Nehemiah and Ezra, the word "Jew" or "Judean" had simply racial and nationalistic significance.

The word, Israel, became the symbol of people who saw themselves as the elect of God. "Now therefore, if you will obey my voice, and keep my covenant, you shall be my own possession among all people; for all the earth is mine, and you shall be to me a kingdom of priests, and a holy nation" (Exodus 19:4-6).

But the elect of God, a kingdom of priests, and a holy nation were not a perfect people. They were not morally pure in observing the stipulations of the covenant, nor were they morally perfect in contrast to the moral level of their neighbors. As a pilgrim people their journey was not only in pursuit of a land of promise, but was also a professional trek through a wilderness of sin and suffering toward their maturation as a light to the nations and a people whose seed would bring unmatched blessings to all nations. Hence, the themes of sin and suffering have their logical place for homiletical development.

Sin, in Old Testament thinking, is that which damages the covenant between persons and between persons and God. Sin cannot take place in isolation. Sin always affects another person or a group of persons as well as the relationship with God. Sin is inclusive of personal and social dimensions because of the nature of interpersonal relationships. Sin can be the failure in relationships of a person, clan, tribe, institution, or nation. The idea of sin extended to every area of life. It was personal and social in terms of human failure. Sin had to do not only with the breaking of ritualistic codes but also with injustice toward the neighbor, widow, or orphan.

Sin, in Old Testament thinking, had a relationship to suffering. In the early chapters of Genesis, suffering appears only after the fall of Adam and Eve. Read Genesis 3:1-16. Suffering seemed to have been a part of the condition of sinful humans and was a sign of chaos which resulted from human rebellion against God. Although the book of Job did not fully solve the mystery of the suffering of the innocent, Isaiah 40—54 suggests that the suffering of the righteous had redemptive and expiatory value for others. In other words, the suggestion is that suffering, like sin, does not take place in isolation. Suffering, as sin, affects the community of persons and the community of persons and God. Whereas sin can lead the human community to its loss, suffering helps to bring the community nearer to its salvation.[26]

26. Consider here the greatest suffering. Early Christian writers often saw the cross through the theology of Isaiah 40 through 54, that is, not merely Jesus as the victim of violence, but also Jesus as the victor over sin, which victory was accomplished through the suffering love of Christ on the cross. Thus, it is through suffering by which salvation may ultimately be achieved.

Related to the mystery of suffering as set forth in the book of Job is the concept of wisdom. In fact, some scholars refer to Job as part of the wisdom literature of the Bible. For in Job the wisdom of God is the perfection of God's knowledge, and it transcends superbly the finite knowledge of persons. (See Job 10:4, 11:6-9, 26:6, and 31:4.) Wisdom studies are also found in Proverbs and Ecclesiastes and in the apocryphal literature of the Bible. Tobit 3:11 and Baruch 3:32-35 relate wisdom to creation. Ben Sira 43 and Wisdom of Solomon 7:17-20, 22-23, and 14:25-26 relate wisdom to geographical, cosmological, and meteorological phenomena. Many shared points of view with biblical wisdom literature can be found in the Egyptian, Babylonian, and other Near Eastern wisdom literature. The idea of wisdom dealt with life experience that had been organized into a practical philosophy of life. Wisdom sought to find some rational meaning for the irrational aspects of living. Wisdom literature was pragmatic and did not build upon ritualistic or cultic religion. This does not mean that wisdom writers denied the sovereignty of God nor did they fail to find the ways of God mysterious and inscrutable. "The fear of the Lord is the beginning of wisdom" (Proverbs 1:7, RSV).

Wisdom writers saw wisdom as a distinct reality outside of Jehovah who first established reason or wisdom at the time when all things were planned. Interesting reading on this point can be found in Proverbs. Proverbs 8:22-26 speaks of the pre-earthly existence of wisdom:

> The Lord created me at the beginning of his work, the first of his acts of old. Ages ago, I was set up, at the first, before the beginning of the earth. When there was no depths I was brought forth, when there were no springs abounding with water. Before the mountains had been shaped, before the hills, I was brought forth, before he had made the earth with its fields, or the first of the dust of the world (Proverbs 8:22-26, RSV).

Wisdom's most perfect human specimen was King Solomon, who did not always use it. Read 1 Kings 3:12. It seems that alongside of the priest and the prophet there was a class for the wise. Read Jeremiah 18:18. The encyclopedic nature of the wisdom of Solomon is illustrated in 1 Kings 4:29-34. The universal appeal, practical nature, and broad truth of wisdom literature place Solomon along with the narrative, historical, priestly, prophetic, legalistic, and intuitive or mystical genres of Scripture. However, preachers must remember the limitations of human wisdom:

> Let not the wise man glory in his wisdom, let not the mighty man glory in his might, let not the rich man glory in his riches; but let him who glories, glory in this, that he understands and knows me, that I am the Lord (Jeremiah 9:23-24, RSV).

Dr. Samuel Proctor shows a sophisticated understanding of textual genre in his apt and artistic use of Proverbs 3:5 in a sermon on "Fear: The Enemy of Faith." Dr. Proctor describes the differences between secular wisdom and divine wisdom. In clear and conversational English, he makes his point in such a way that the untrained ear and eye could easily miss the distinction between conventional and biblical wisdom, yet the point of the proclamation is clear:

> You see, conventional wisdom says play it safe. Don't take any chances. But a wisdom beyond our own says, "Trust in the Lord with all thine heart, and lean not unto thine own understanding" (Proverbs 3:5, KJV).[27]

Dr. Proctor reminds us that contemporary concerns need to be addressed by the preacher with the searching and critical message of biblical wisdom literature. Each person in the pew, irrespective of age or academic or gender classification will be deeply touched as the preacher probes the depths of human existence in relationship to the theological insights hidden in the wisdom literature of the Old Testament. The best expression of the

---

27. Samuel D. Proctor and William E. Watley, *From the Black Pulpit*, (Valley Forge, PA: Judson Press, 1985), p. 75.

theology of wisdom literature that I have read has been framed as an argument in search of Divine Presence:

> God's presence is not automatic, despite a desire to be known. Dame Wisdom calls, invites, celebrates with her guests, but she also threatens those who show no appreciation for her wares. She must compete with Madame Folly, whose power to destroy remains hidden until the last second. Unfortunately, those who treasure God's presence cannot count on continued blessing. Virtue does not always bring divine presence in its wake. Good people sometimes experience divine absence, however much they long for His presence. Such withdrawal may constitute a test, or it may defy explanation.[28]

28. James L. Crenshaw, "In Search of Divine Presence; Some Remarks Preliminary to a Theology of Wisdom, Old Testament Theology," *Review and Expositor*, Vol. LXXIV, No. 3, Louisville, KY, Summer 1977, p. 366.

CHAPTER FOUR
Preaching the Old Testament Books

In the Hebrew Bible the title for Psalms is *tehillim*. This term simply means songs of praise. Early Christians who read the Greek version of the Old Testament, commonly called the Septuagint, used the Greek word *psalmos* as a title for the Psalms. This title comes from Luke 20:42 and Acts 1:20. Through the years, scholars have come to refer to the Psalms as the Psalter.

Preachers would do well to study Old Testament psalms that are not included in the quintuple Psalter. These include the song of the sea (Exodus 15:1-18), the song of Miriam (Exodus 15:20-21), the song of Moses (Deuteronomy 32:1-43), the song of Deborah (Judges 5:1-31), the song of Hannah (1 Samuel 2:1-10), David's song of deliverance (2 Samuel 22:2-51), a song of thanksgiving (Isaiah 12:4-6), King Hezekiah's songs (Isaiah 38:9-20), the prayer of Habakkuk (Habakkuk 3:2-19), Jonah's prayer (Jonah 2:2-9), the prophetic hymns of Isaiah (Isaiah 42:10-12, 52:9-10), the hymns of Job (Job 5:8-16, 9:4-10, 12:7-10, 12:13-25), and Job's songs of lament (3:3-12, 13-19, 20-26, 7:1-10, 7:12-21; 9:25-31, 10:1-22). The preaching of the psalms of lament in Jeremiah can find a focus in Jeremiah 15:15-18, 17:14-18, 18:19-23, and, assuming no objection to Jeremiah as the author of Lamentations, Lamentations 3—5. Other psalms are found in the literature of the Apocrypha in Ecclesiasticus or the Wisdom of Jesus 51:1-12 and in Tobit 13.

Scholars tell us that the Psalter is the hymn book of the second temple or the temple of Zerubbabel which was rebuilt in 520-515 B.C. Prophets Haggai and Zechariah were serving during this time. Some scholars believe that the rise of the synagogues, which kept the faith of Israel alive in those newly founded Jewish colonies out of Palestine, depended largely upon the use of the Psalter as a book of songs and prayers. The Greek Old Testament contains Psalm 151 which is not a part of the Hebrew Old Testament that the Protestant founding fathers and mothers used.

Scholars also tell us that the five-fold structure of the Psalter is patterned after the Pentateuch or the first five books of the Old Testament. This structure is as follows:

Book One—Psalms 1—41.
Book Two—Psalms 42-72.
Book Three—Psalms 73—89.
Book Four—Psalms 90—106.
Book Five—Psalms 107-150.

Those who preach from the Psalms would do well to remember that Psalms 1 and 2 are key psalms with two key theological themes. The necessity of meditating upon the Law is the first theme. The hope for the Messiah to return to inaugurate God's Kingdom is the second theme.

Two scholars important in helping others to interpret the Psalms are German scholar Hermann Gunkel and Scandinavian scholar Sigmund Mowinckel. Gunkel and Mowinckel have brought a "form-critical" approach to the study of the Psalter. This approach stresses the point that psalms must be classified or identified according to literary type. Literary teachers would use the word "genre." This means that readers must ask, when they read a psalm, if the psalm is praising, thanking, lamenting, repenting, narrating, instructing, confessing, or testifying in the presence of God. It is important for preachers to consider the form of a psalm. The knowledge of the form is helpful as form must be related to the situation in which the form functions. For example, some psalms may have an Easter theme implicit in their context when another mood may be needed. Preachers will be required to search for psalms that speak to the emotional needs of the worship service. Persons interested in learning more about classifying psalms should read *The Psalms: A Form-Critical Introduction*, Fortress Press, Facet Books, 1967, written by Hermann Gunkel. The role of the Psalms in the cult can be further explored by reading Sigmund Mowin-ckel's *Psalms in Israel's Worship*, Volumes 1-3, translated by D. R. Ap-Thomas, Abingdon Press, 1962.

There can be no denial of the Canaanite influence upon the Psalms. This does not mean that the Israelites stole religious content and theology from their Canaanite neighbors. On the contrary, it means that they used the existing Canaanite rituals and communication forms to transmit to their neighbors their powerful faith in Yahweh. You may ask how that happened. The process started when the Israelites settled in Canaan, possibly two hundred years before David's kingship. Upon locating on the land, the Israelites became aware of Canaanite sanctuaries in places like Shechem, Bethel, Shiloh, and Jerusalem. In Hebrew, *Beth* means house and *El* means the high god of the Canaanite pantheon. However, the Israelites appropriated the term *El* as well as the three great agricultural festivals of the Canaanites, sacrifice as an external form of worship, and the psalm as a literary form. The pilgrimages to the religious festivals coincided with the major agricultural seasons. For example, the Festival of Unleavened Bread (later associated with the Passover) was held in March to April at the time of the barley harvest; the second, the Festival of First Fruits (also called Weeks or Pentecost), occurred in May and June at the time of the wheat harvest; and the third, the Festival of Ingathering (also called Tabernacles), took place in September and October at the time of the olive and grape harvests.

A most important event was Rosh Hashanah. It was an old Canaanite wine festival that became a New Year's Day celebration. On that day there was dancing and fun time. According to Judges 21:19-23, the following took place:

So they said, Behold there is a yearly feast of the Lord at

Shiloh, which is north of Bethel, on the east of the
highway that goes up from Bethel to Shechem, and south
of Lebonah. And they commanded the Benjamites saying,
Go and lie in wait in the vineyards, and watch if the
daughters of Shiloh come out to dance in the dances, then
come out of the vineyards and seize each man his wife
from the daughters of Shiloh, and go to the land of Benjamin and when their fathers or their brothers come to
complain to us, we will say to them, Grant them gracious-
ly to us; because we did not take each man of them his
wife in battle, neither did you give them to them, else you
now would be guilty. And the Benjamites did so, and took
their wives, according to their number, from the dancers
whom they carried off; then they went and returned to
their inheritance, and rebuilt the towns and dwelt in them
(Judges 21:19-23, RSV).

At the time of this festival, Hannah came to the temple with a
heavy heart. She was so burdened that she could not pray audibly.
Eli, the priest, misjudged Hannah and wrongly accused her of
drunkenness. This account comes to us from 1 Samuel 1:1-19. This
festival, which called for merriment, was transformed into an event
in which Israel would remember its abode in the wilderness. In the
wilderness the Israelites lived in huts or shelters During the
festival, which continues to this day, the Israelites made huts or
shelters out of tree branches and erected them in the vineyards
while the grapes were harvested.

According to 1 King 12:32-33, a harvest festival or feast of the
tabernacles was established for those persons in the north who
were under the rule of Jeroboam I. This king, who ruled from
931-910 B.C., did not want Israel or Ephraim to make their
pilgrimage to the temple in Jerusalem. So he made Bethel the site
of their pilgrimage for the fall festival. One of the psalms used at
this feast was a community lament found in Psalm 80:8-11:

Thou didst bring a vine out of Egypt; thou didst drive out
the nations and plant it. Thou didst clear the ground for

it; it took a deep root and filled the land. The mountains were covered with its shade, the mighty cedars with its branches, to the sea, and its shoots to the river (Psalm 80:8-11, RSV).

The covenant renewal service was based on Joshua 24. An outline of the service includes eight components:

1. The call to assembly (Joshua 24:1).
2. Historical prologue (Joshua 24:2-13).
3. Call to decision for or against Yahweh (Joshua 24:14-22).
4. Purification: removal of foreign gods (Joshua 24:23-24).
5. The renewal of the covenant (Joshua 24:25; Exodus 24:4-8).
6. The reading of the covenant law (Joshua 24:25-26; Exodus 24:7).
7. A ceremony of sanctions: the blessings and the curses (Deuteronomy 27:11-26; Joshua 8:30-35).
8. The dismissal of the congregation (Joshua 24:28).[29]

Along with covenant renewal psalms are the narrative or storytelling psalms such as 105, 106, 135, 136; psalms of individual laments such as 5, 7, 9-10, 17, 26, 27:7-14, 52; psalms of community laments, 12, 44, 58, 60, 90, 94, 123, 129; psalms of thanksgiving, 18, 21, 30, 32, 34, 40:1-11, 66:13-20, wisdom psalms, 36, 37, 49, 73, 112; enthronement psalms, 24, 29, 47, 93, 95, 96, 97, 98, 99, and psalms of trust such as 11, 16, 23, 27, 46, 62, 90, and 121. The temple psalms, also called songs of Zion, include psalms 48, 76, 84, 87, and 122.

Preachers will increase their appreciation of the psalms as they become more aware of the literary devices used to give them poetic beauty. One literary device that makes use of repetition is called parallelism. There are different kinds of parallelism. Examples are as follows:

---

29. Bernhard W. Anderson, *Out of the Depths: The Psalms Speak to Us Today*, (Philadelphia: Westminster, 1983), pp. 169-70.

1. *Synonymous parallelism* occurs when the second line of a couplet repeats the thought in the first line.

   "My God, my God, why hast thou forsaken me? Why art thou so far from helping me, from the words of my groaning?" (Psalm 22:1, RSV).

2. *Antithetical parallelism* takes place when the second line of a couplet presents an idea different from the thought in the first line.

   "Many are rising against me. Many are saying of me, there is no help for him in God. But thou, O Lord, art a shield about me, my glory and the lifter of my head" (Psalm 3:2-3, RSV).

3. *Synthetic parallelism* occurs when the two lines of a couplet are only loosely attached, but the second line completes or adds to the meaning of the first line.

   "Thou hast put more joy in my heart, than they have when their grain and wine abound" (Psalm 4:7, RSV).

4. *Emblematic parallelism* occurs when a line presents as a simile the thought of the other.

   "As far as the east is from the west, so far does He remove our transgressions from us" (Psalm 103:12, RSV).

5. *Stairlike parallelism* takes place when there is a continuing development of a part of a line in the second and third lines.

   "Bless the Lord, all His hosts, His ministers that do His will. Bless the Lord, all His works, in all places of His dominion; Bless the Lord, O my soul" (Psalm 103:21-22, RSV).

6. *Introverted parallelism:*

   "*We have escaped* as a bird from the snare of the fowlers; The snare is broken and *we have escaped*" (Psalm 124:7, RSV).[30]

---

30. Leonard L. Thompson, *Introducing Biblical Literature*, (Englewood Cliffs: Prentice Hall, 1978), pp. 18-19.

The triplet or tristich is seen in Psalm 93:3:
"The floods have lifted up, Yahweh,
the floods have lifted up their voice;
the floods lift up their roaring."
The tetratich of four lines is expressed in Psalm 55:21:
"His mouth was smooth as butter,
but war was in his heart;
Softer than oil his words,
yet were they drawn swords."
The penastich of five lines is as follows in Psalm 6:6-7:
"I am weary with my moaning;
every night I flood my bed with tears,
I drench my couch with my weeping.
My eye wastes away because of grief;
it grows weak because of all my foes."
The hexastich of six lines appears in Psalm 99:1-3:
"The Lord reigns; let the people tremble!
He sits enthroned upon the cherubim; let the earth
quake!
The Lord is great in Zion;
He is exalted over all the peoples.
Let them praise thy great and terrible name.
Holy is he."

After understanding the literary structure of the Psalms, preachers can study the Psalms for their theological significance. For example, the concept of messiah in the Psalms is a good place for Christian pastors to begin understanding how messiahship had a different meaning than in the New Testament. The difference in meaning should not shock some preachers because Professor John I. Durham has written about the five dimensions of Holy Scripture. These dimensions should be memorized and used by pastors as they approach texts such as those which discuss the idea of messiah. Said Dr. Durham regarding the dimensions of Holy Scripture:

The first of these we may call the width, for convenience;

it represents the span of a concept in his own context, what a given psalmist meant when he spoke of messiah. The second dimension, the height, represents the extent of that concept beyond its specific usage in a given passage—what did messiah mean to the people who first sang the psalms. The third dimension, the depth, represents the broader range of the concept through the whole of the Old Testament and even the Bible—who and what is messiah in the exilic period, or during the ministry of Jesus, or when the church burst suddenly into visible life like a flame too long smoldering?

But there is also a fourth dimension of Holy Scriptures and a fifth. The fourth dimension we may call the time of the concept, its range of application across the years that have elapsed since its genesis, a light that may reach a later age after the source generating it has changed, and a light that is perceived in specific relation to the setting in which it is received. The fifth dimension of Holy Scripture, on this analogy, would be the transcendent dimension, the space of the infinite pattern, the idea as God Himself conceived it and thinks it, the limitless dimension without dimensions by comparison with the width, height, depth, and time of our imperfect perceptions of the perfect concept.[31]

Failure to employ the dimensions articulated by Durham may lead to exegesis and irresponsible conclusions. For example, messiah in the psalms always speaks of the ruling king. This king was God's appointed and anointed. Yet preachers often preach these texts as references to Jesus Christ. Scholars talk about the idea of sacral kingship that is instituted by God. Only God is the permanent King. So, then, a difference must be made between sacral kingship and divine kingship. Sacral kingship depends upon divine kingship. Psalm 89 celebrates the certainty of God's promise

31. John I. Durham, "The King as Messiah in the Psalms, *Review and Expositor*, Vol. LXXXI, No. 3, Louisville, KY, Summer 1984, pp. 425-426.

to the Davidic king while Psalm 2 deals with God's guarantee of the authority of the Davidic king.

The omnipresence and omniscience of God are theologically clear in Psalm 139. The author makes it clear to all that God is not limited by space or time or in intelligence. Read Psalm 139:

> O Lord thou hast searched me and known me! Thou knowest when I sit down and when I rise up; thou discernest my thoughts from afar. Thou searchest out my path and my lying down, and art acquainted with all my ways. Even before a word is on my tongue, lo, O Lord, thou knowest it altogether. Thou dost beset me behind and before, and layest thy hand upon me. Such knowledge is too wonderful for me; it is so high I cannot attain to it. Whither shall I go from thy Spirit? Or whither shall I flee from thy presence? If I ascend to heaven, thou art there. If I make my bed in sheol, thou art there. If I take the wings of morning and dwell in the uttermost part of the sea, even there thy hand shall lead me and thy right hand shall hold me (Psalm 139:10, RSV).

The theological theme of trust is seen in Psalm 27:1: "The Lord is my light and my salvation: whom shall I fear? The Lord is the stronghold of my life; of whom shall I be afraid." Fellowship and communion with God are apparent in Psalm 42:1: "As a heart longs for flowing streams, so longs my soul for thee, O God. My soul thirsts for God, for the living God."

Themes of repentance and forgiveness are clear in Psalm 51:1-2, 10-12:

> "Have mercy on me, O God, according to thy steadfast love; according to thy abundant mercy blot out my transgressions. Wash me thoroughly from my iniquity, and cleanse me from my sin.
>
> Create in me a clean heart, O God, and put a new and right spirit within me. Cast me not away from thy presence and take not thy Holy Spirit from me. Restore

unto me the joy of thy salvation, and uphold me with a
willing spirit."

The belief of the Hebrew people in the law had great
theological significance. The Torah had a dominating role in the
life of the Hebrew people. Their intense love of the law was the
basis for the controlling power of the law in guiding their moral
and ceremonial practices. The law led them to God and godly living. The reverence of the law provided them with a canon for living with reverence in the presence of God. The attitude of many
Jews and Christians in holding the Scriptures in such high esteem
is expressed in Psalm 19:7-10:

> The law of the Lord is perfect, reviving the soul; the
> testimony of the Lord is sure, making wise the simple; the
> precepts of the Lord are right, rejoicing the heart; the com-
> mandments of the Lord are pure, enlightening the eyes;
> the fear of the Lord is clean, enduring forever; the or-
> dinances of the Lord are true, and righteous altogether.
> More to be desired are they than gold, even much fine
> gold; sweeter also than honey, and the drippings of the
> honeycomb.

Too many times the theological mandate for the election of
Israel is ignored by preachers. This is because many persons believe
that Israel and modern-day Jews are egocentric in their messianic
message. They argue that the missionary motif of appealing to and
reaching non-Jews was absent from the theology of Israel. Psalm 67
decries this point of view.

> May God be gracious to us and bless us and make his face
> to shine upon us that thy way may be known upon earth,
> thy saving power among all nations. Let the peoples praise
> thee, O God; let all the peoples praise thee.
> Let the nations be glad and sing for joy, for thou dost
> judge the peoples with equity and guide the nations upon
> earth. Let the peoples praise thee, O God; let all the
> peoples praise thee!

The earth has yielded its increase; God, our God, has blessed us. God has blessed us. Let all the ends of the earth fear him! (Psalm 67, RSV).

Thy word is a lamp to guide my feet and a light on my path; I have bound myself by oath and solemn vow to keep thy just decrees (Psalm 119:9, 11, 105-106, NEB).

The Psalms are very popular texts for preachers in the Black church tradition. Because the Psalms address the full array of human emotions and experiences, they provide rich homiletical resources. Preachers can find spiritual good for their own devotional lives and for life-situation preaching in a serious study of the Psalms.

In using the Psalms in a sermon entitled "The Eyes of the Lord," Leotis Belk said:

Wherever God looks—which is everywhere—God sheds light. For in Him is light, and He is the light not only of men but also of stones and rocks, gnats and flies, alligators and rattlesnakes, fire and smoke, bacillus and capillaries, rubber bands and fabric—a thousand things. Our manufacturing things in the world does not change God's seeing what they are. If we would but reflect on it, we might find that God led us to our seeing.

He that planted the ear shall he not hear?

He that formed the eye shall he not see? (Psalm 94:9, KJV).[32]

In preaching from Psalm 102:6, "I am like a pelican of the wilderness, I am like an owl of the desert," Henry C. Gregory III says:

There is the loneliness of displacement in which one is out of his natural habitat. A New Yorker may be with people in Stafford County, Virginia, and still feel lonely. The

32. Leotis Belk, "The Eyes of the Lord," *Outstanding Black Sermons*, J. Alfred Smith, ed., (Valley Forge, PA: Judson Press, 1976, fourth printing, 1983), p. 10.

farmer may be on a crowded street in Chicago and feel very much alone.[33]

In *Rules for the Road,* Harry S. Wright masterfully gives an exposition on the Psalms. He argues:

> I want to read a few words from the lips of a man who has found a way to keep his feet firmly planted on the ground of reality, one who has found joy that brings into his life both light and life, one who has discovered something that holds him steady and brings him through. He begins with a question directed straight to the young.
>
> How shall a young man steer a (steady) course?
>
> His answer to this good question follows in the same breath: By holding to thy word, I treasure thy promise in my heart, for fear that I might sin against thee.[34]

Proverbs

According to 1 Kings 4:32, Solomon knew three thousand proverbs and his songs were one thousand and five. Nonetheless, scholars argue that other authors contributed to the collection of proverbs that comprise the book of Proverbs. Grecian and Egyptian influence as well as Aramaic words are manifested in Proverbs. The last two chapters of Proverbs are by Agur and Lemuel. These wise persons are unknown authors. Although Solomon may have spoken three thousand proverbs, only eight hundred of his proverbs are included in the book that bears his name.

As clearly stated in chapter one, moral discretion and clear perception constitute the purpose of the book of Proverbs whereas the fear of God looms as its theme. In a modern context, Proverbs is an excellent manual on Christian ethics as it pertains to personal discipline and private morality. The personification of wisdom in

33. Henry C. Gregory, III, "The Shepherd," *Outstanding Black Sermons,* J. Alfred Smith, ed., (Valley Forge, PA: Judson Press, 1976, fourth printing, 1983), p. 35.

34. Op. cit., p. 91.

Proverbs reminds preachers of Christ of the wisdom of God as portrayed in the Colossian letter.

Ecclesiastes

Preachers in the modern world meet countless persons who suffer from ennui. Empty lives and purposelessness are expressed in existential literature and in plays and drama. The skepticism and pessimistic philosophies of this century make it necessary for preachers to carefully examine the theology of Ecclesiastes.

Some theological principles in Ecclesiastes include:

1. *The Sovereignty of God*
   Ecclesiastes 6:2; 7:13; 9:1.
2. *God's Justice*
   Ecclesiastes 5:8; 8:12-13.
3. *Human Sinfulness*
   Ecclesiastes 7:20; 9:3.
4. *Immortality*
   Ecclesiastes 3:11; 12:7.
5. *God's Punishment and Rewards*
   Ecclesiastes 2:26; 3:17; 8:12; 11:9; 12:14.

At funerals, some preachers have preached from Ecclesiastes 3:11:

He has also set eternity in the hearts of men; yet they cannot fathom what God has done from beginning to the end (NIV).

The Song of Songs

Very few sermons are preached from the Song of Songs. Perhaps it is because the book seems to be secular literature that makes no use of theological language or religious symbolism. The name of God appears nowhere in the book. Modern Christians with a long puritanical legacy may be embarrassed by the bold metaphors, extravagant imagery, and sexual overtones that are replete in the book.

This response to the Song of Songs was the basis for controversy among early Jewish scholars. The Palestinian School of Shammai was against including the book in the canon whereas the Babylonian school of Hillel favored its inclusion.

Scholars have had great differences on the proper interpretation of the Song of Songs. In the Mishnah, Talmud, and Targums, Jewish writers have said that the Song represents God's love for Israel. Christian scholars have done a similar thing. They have written about Christ's love of the church and about the church's love for Christ. Some argue that the song is a drama in which King Solomon falls in love with a Shulamite girl and takes her to his capital in Jerusalem. His love was purified from sensual to pure love. Still other persons see the picture of the Shulamite girl as true to her shepherd husband in spite of the temptations of Solomon. Scholars have also seen the Song of Songs as a collection of love songs. Jews have found liturgical use for the book. They have read the book on the eighth day of the Passover celebration at the genesis of the new year. Some Scriptures in the book lend themselves to preaching texts. A few examples are:

1:6	"They made me keeper of the vineyards: but my own vineyard, I have not kept."
2:4	"He brought me to the banqueting house, and his banner over me was love."
2:11-12	"For lo, the winter is past, the time of singing has come."
2:15	"Catch us the foxes, the little foxes."
5:2	"I slept, but my heart was awake."
8:6	"Set me as a seal upon your heart, as a seal upon your heart, for love is strong as death."
8:7	"Many waters cannot quench love, neither can floods drown it."
1:5	"I am black, but comely, O ye daughters of Jerusalem, as the tents of Kedar, as the curtains of Solomon."
8:14	"Make haste, my beloved, and be like a gazelle or a young stag upon the mountains of spices."

Preachers with no music in their soul and no poetic vibrations in their heart will have great difficulty preaching from the Song of Songs. In a sensate culture where love is often defined as the human response to glandular secretions, there is a need for Christian preaching that will portray agape love that God has expressed to human kind in Jesus Christ. Preaching from the Song of Songs can open the door for preachers to contrast God's love with the sickly expressions of false love that are depicted in the mass media.

Job

The book of Job mirrors the crisis in the life of a person who lost wealth, health, family, and community status. Catastrophe after catastrope brought Job to his knees. The question that surfaced was "Why?" "Why do the good suffer?" Three friends of Job, Eliphaz, Bildad, and Zophar, attempted to speak to the issue of suffering and providence. When their speeches ended in a pathetic deadlock with Job, young Elihu suddenly entered into the discussion. In the final analysis, God entered the discussion and silenced each of the speakers and humbled Job who had become self-righteous and bitter.

Job's major complaints were threefold. First of all, God did not hear him. (See Job 13:3, 24, 19:7, 23:3-5, and 30:20.) Secondly, God was punishing him, and seemingly without cause. (See Job 6:4, 7:20, and 9:17.) Thirdly, God allowed wicked persons to prosper. (See Job 21:7.) Job was also sorry that he was ever born. (See Job 1:21 and 2:10.)

Eliphaz, the Temanite, was the eldest of the speakers. He addressed Job three times, first in Job 4:3-7 and then in Job 15. The third speech was in Job 22. Eliphaz based his arguments on observation and spiritual revelation. (See Job 4:8 and Job 4:12-16.)

Bildad, the Shuite, was the voice of tradition. He also gave three speeches. In chapters 8, 18, and 25, he gave an appeal, a rebuke, and an evasion. He was severe and arrogant in criticizing Job.

Zophar, the Naamathite, spoke only twice. (See chapter 11 and chapter 20 for curt and cutting speeches based on assumption.)

Elihu was the youngest of all the speakers. He spoke last but was very lengthy. (See chapters 32—37.) Elihu had a more informed understanding of suffering than Job's three friends. For him, suffering was not just to chastise, but to chasten. Elihu held a redemptive concept of suffering's purpose. With knowledge beyond his years, Elihu advised Job to suffer with humility rather than with protestation.

After God spoke to Job in chapter 38:1-18, Job experienced a personal encounter with God that was humbling and life-transforming. Indeed, Job learned to live with unanswered questions and to trust God with the mysteries of life, including the mysteries in his own.

The Pentateuchal Documents

The understanding of Israel's development as a nation enables one to preach from the Old Testament with a sense of historical integrity. The story of Israel is discovered in the first five books of the Bible, which are called the Torah in the Jewish tradition. Christians refer to these books as either the Law or the Pentateuch. The prophetic books of the Bible give clarity to the Pentateuch, and the historical, poetic, or wisdom books of the Bible provide meditations, reflections, or a midrash on the Pentateuch.

Serious biblical scholarship cannot overlook the metamorphosis or growth of the Pentateuch. Scholars agree that several originally separate documents which were composed in different periods of history have been harmonized into the present body of Scripture.

Undergirding the concept of pentateuchal traditions are several convictions such as:

1. The influence of the personality of Moses in the literature.
2. Stories, speeches, laws, meditations, liturgical celebrations, and other units of literature were transmitted by oral traditions for a number of years.

3. At different times scribes, wise persons, priests, and prophets collected these units of oral and written literature and four distinct traditions or documents emerged.

4. These documents or traditions became a single five volume work, perhaps around 400 A.D., under the influence of Ezra.

These four main documents are designated by the letters J, E, D, and P. The easiest of the documents to identify is D because it consists of, for the most part, the book of Deuteronomy. The priestly or P document is easily recognized because of its emphasis and elaboration of genealogies and the origins of Israel's sacred festivities and institutions. The J document can be identified for its emphasis upon the tribe of Judah in the south and for its use of Yahweh or Jehovah as the name of God. The E document places emphasis upon the tribe of Ephraim in the northern part of Israel and uses the name of Elohim for God. In Genesis 37 there is a fusion of J and E traditions. Some scholars call this J.E.

That part of the Genesis 37 narrative which tells us that Joseph was cast into a pit to die but was saved by Midianites who took him to Egypt where they sold him into slavery is from the E source. The E source also credits Reuben with saving Joseph from death. But the J source depicts Judah as having saved Joseph. By interweaving the two originally separate documents, the redactor harmonizes two sources which both carry a historical core of truth that completes to the best possible extent the full core of the history of the narrative.

These four traditions were collected in a single volume called the Pentateuch. This work was finished about 400 A.D., and its authorship has often been attributed to Ezra. Each tradition is distinctly characterized.

The J or Yahwist was excellent as a storyteller. His stories were vivid. He presented God as a man who, in the creation story, was a gardner, potter, surgeon, and toiler. He was a friend to Abraham. He spoke to Abraham with commands and addressed Adam with prohibitions. He is always ready to forgive sinful persons. He is eager to renew His blessings with human kind.

The E or Elohist tradition depicts God in elevated language. As a transcendent being, God speaks to humans through theophanies or mystical manifestations. God is a holy and moral God who sends prophets to speak for Himself. He is a God of law or a God of the covenant traditions.

The D or Deuteronomist tradition emphasizes God as the One who has chosen Israel to be His people. He has given them land and commandments to keep. Israel must be faithful to God. Israel must hear and heed the commandments.

The P or priestly tradition is formal. Repetition is characteristic of priestly writers. Genealogies and technical cult language appear. Worship has prominence in priestly writings. The priesthood as an institution is described. Priestly writers describe the creation story in Genesis 1. God's holiness and the necessity of blood sacrifice are stressed along with religious festivals.

The J and P traditions are concerned with beginnings in Genesis 1—11, and the J.E.P. traditions deal with the patriarchs in Genesis 12—50. These same traditions develop Exodus 1—15 in describing the departure from Egypt and in narrating the wilderness experiences in Exodus 16—18. The E tradition is found in Exodus 19—24. Exodus 25—31 describes the priestly tradition of the Covenant, followed by J.E. traditions in Exodus 32—34. Chapters 35—40 are one with Leviticus and Numbers 1—10 in being priestly in nature. Numbers 11—12 come from the J.E. sources and Numbers 13—36 are a mixture of J.E.P. sources while Deuteronomy is exclusively from the Deuteronomic tradition. In all of these Pentateuch documents, Moses and Abraham are the principal characters.

For preaching purposes, the Pentateuch should be viewed as a portrayal of five related theological strands.

1. Genesis: The birth of the nation of Israel.
2. Exodus: The bondage and liberation of the nation of Israel by God.
3. Leviticus: The worship of God by the nation of Israel.

4. Numbers: The testing of the nation of Israel by God.
5. Deuteronomy: The law of God for the nation of Israel.

Scholars say that a portion of Deuteronomy may be the book of the law mentioned in 2 Kings 22—23 which was the basis of the reforms of Josiah in 622 or 623. Some say that although Deuteronomy is based upon ancient tradition, it is a reinterpretation of Mosaic teaching in the light of later historical understanding.

The Deuteronomic Code is found in chapters 12—16:29. A beautiful theology is expressed in verses 26:5-10, "A wondering Aramean was my father. . ." (RSV). The covenant renewal and Moses' last discourse and death are found in chapters 27—50.

The Historical Traditions

Joshua

Scholars are concerned about the complexity of the composite of many sources in the book of Joshua. Some of the material is poetry and some of the material is prose. The discussion of the J and E traditions do not show agreement in the scholarly community. Scholars believe that some narratives report oral traditions about Gilgal and Shechem, and that they are etiological in purpose as they explain the origins of customs and the parameters of tribal boundaries. Some scholars attribute the denomination of certain cities for the conquests mentioned in Joshua to the working of Deuteronomic editors because of historical resources that indicate that the actual origin of the cities postdate the conquests which were to have taken place in them. The territory prophesied to be conquered was far more extensive than the empire of David.

In any event, for preaching purposes the book could be simply outlined as:

Entering the land—1-5.
Conquering the Land—6-12.
Occupying the land—13-24.

Some scholars think that Joshua could properly end at chapter

23 and that assembly at Shechem and the accounting of Joshua's death in chapter 24 could be an appendix. They also believe that the tribes of Leah, Reuben, Simeon, Levi, and Judah, who had not been a part of the Exodus and desert wanderings, were challenged in chapter 24 to live faithfully pursuant to the demands of the covenant.

Judges

The Hebrew word for Judges is *shofet*. It means military leader or deliverer. Six major and six minor judges appear as leaders who emerge as deliverers in the time of acute crisis. Some of the judges served concurrently rather than in a chronological succession. In some situations a tribe would win a battle in isolation. In other instances the tribes would unite to defeat the enemy. The conquest of Canaan reported in Judges 1—2:5 is not as optimistic as the report in Joshua. Some of the conquest efforts reported in Judges were partially successful. For example, the tribe of Naphtali did not drive the Canaanites from the land. They lived in the land with the Canaanites, using them as a forced labor group.

Professor Duane Christensen of the American Baptist Seminary of the West in Berkeley, California has helped me to appreciate the powerful presence of women leaders in Judges such as Deborah and Jael. These persons provide worthy topics for biographical preaching. Other topics for biographical preaching are Othniel, 3:7-11; Ehud, 3:12-30; Shamgar, 3:31; Gideon, 6—8; Abimelech, 9; Tola and Jair, 10:1-5; Jephthah, 10:6—12:7.

The sacrifice of Jephthah's daughter reminds literary-minded persons of the female sacrifice of Iphigenia by Agamemnon in the Grecian writings of Euripides. (Human sacrifice, however, is condemned in Leviticus 20:2.)

The theological cycle of sin, suffering, supplication, and salvation necessitated a leadership role of the judges in moving the people through crises in their spiritual development.

The book of Judges offers other preaching themes in chapters 13—16, the story of Samson, and in chapters 17—21, the war between Israel and Benjamin.

Ruth

In the Hebrew Bible Ruth is included among the writings. In the Greek text of the Hebrew Bible Ruth was placed after Judges and before Samuel in keeping with the genealogy, indicating that Ruth was David's grandmother. It is the theological conviction of this author that Ruth was composed and placed in the canon to combat the ethnocentrism and racial exclusiveness found in Ezra and Nehemiah. I also believe that this is a basic purpose for the book of Jonah. Hence, I would date both books as post-exilic. However, other writers would disagree.

For preaching purposes, the following outline is presented, which could be developed in a narrative form:

Ruth—The Faithful Daughter.
　　—The Humble Servant.
　　—The Loving Servant.
　　—The Rewarded Servant.

In an age of women's liberation, perhaps it would be acceptable exegesis to say that Ruth 3:9 was a female proposal for marriage. Preachers will, of course, preach this book according to their own training, and theological and thoughtful reflections.

1 Samuel

Originally the books of 1 and 2 Samuel were one book. Before the text was written in Greek, which requires a great deal more space, the Hebrew text could contain the material in one document. Scholars have indicated that a number of independent units have formed the data for the books of Samuel. This material came from worship centers at Mizpah, Shiloh, and Gilgal and from oral traditions about Samuel, Saul, and David.

The court history of David which some scholars refer to as the Succession Document provided material for 2 Samuel 9—20 and 1 Kings 1—2. There seems to have been a syncretism of the Saul source and the Samuel source. The Samuel source was a later source which was the antithesis of the Saul source in that it was anti-monarchy, anti-Saul, and more favorable to Samuel as the judge and true leader of Israel. It was written between 750-650 B.C., whereas the Saul source was composed during the time of King Solomon. 2 Samuel merges the Saul source with the court history or Succession Document.

Milestones which the homiletical eye should observe when reading 1 Samuel are:

1. The first use of the term "Lord of hosts," 1:3.
2. The first use of the term "Messiah," 2:10.
3. The first use of the term "word of the Lord," 3:1.
4. The first use of the word "Ichabod," 4:21.
5. The first use of the word "Ebenezer," 7:12.
6. The first use of the term "God Save the King," 10:24.
7. The first use of the term "seer," 9:9.

Preachers would do well to observe the Holy Spirit of God at work as:

1. The author of a new heart, 10:9.
2. The author of righteous anger, 11:6.

1 Samuel is replete with numerous passages that jump from the page to inspire preachers. The narratives provide attractive biography for preaching. Preachers can preach with ease from 1 Samuel about the disasters of irresponsible parenting, the perils of disobedience, and the futility of empty formalism in worship. The prayer life of Samuel is also an illustrious study for those who make a scrutinizing examination of 1 Samuel.

In preaching from 1 Samuel, preachers will notice three main divisions:

1. Samuel, the Obedient Prophet, 1—7.
2. Saul, the Rejected, 8—15.
3. David, the Anointed King, 16—31.

2 Samuel

This book is a detailed narrative about the death of Saul, David's lament for Saul and Jonathan, David's ascension to the throne, the war between the houses of David and Saul, the crown-

ing of David as king over all of Israel, the establishing of the capital
at Jerusalem, David's defeat of the Philistines, God's promise to
David, David's prayer, David's aspirations, disappointments, kind-
nesses, sins, victories, failures, troubles, last words, mighty men,
census of Israel and Judah, and David's construction of an altar on
the threshing floor of Araunah, the Jebusite. The theme of 2 Samuel could be preached as "The Story of Triumph and Tragedy."

Sermons on 2 Samuel could also be preached from the following themes:

1. Accession, 1—5.
2. Prosperity, 6—10.
3. Adversity, 11-19.
4. Finality, 20—24.

A poetic text for preaching is found in 2 Samuel:

"Your beauty, O Israel, is slain on your high places! How
have the mighty fallen! Tell it not in Gath, Proclaim it not
in the streets of Ashkelon; Lest the daughters of the Philistines rejoice, Lest the daughters of the uncircumcised ex-
ult" (2 Samuel 1:19, 20, NAS).

Some may be moved to preach:

"How have the mighty fallen in the midst of the battle!
Jonathan is slain on your high places. I am distressed for
you, my brother Jonathan; You have been very pleasant
to me. Your love to me was more wonderful than the love
of women. How have the mighty fallen, and the weapons
of war perished!" (2 Samuel 1:25-27, NAS).

A most tender passage that reveals the magnanimity of David
is relevant for contemporary times:

Then David said, "Is there yet anyone left of the house of
Saul, that I may show him kindness for Jonathan's sake?"
(2 Samuel 9:1, NAS).

Or, in preaching to preachers, we might be reminded of Joab's
words to Ahimaaz:

And Joab said, "Why would you run, my son, since you will have no reward for going?" (2 Samuel 18:22b, NAS).

The best-known text for a Father's Day sermon on a parent's broken heart is:

"O my son Absalom, my son, my son Absalom! Would I had died instead of you, O Absalom, my son, my son!" (2 Samuel 18:33b, NAS).

1 Kings

Kings, like Samuel, was originally a single book. The book of Kings is the least part of the Deuteronomic history of Israel from Joshua to the Exile. Kings contains many more sources than Samuel and it reveals a more detailed editing. Some of the source material in Kings came from a lost source called "The Book of the Acts of Solomon" as well as "The Book of the Chronicles of the Kings of Israel" and "The Book of the Chronicles of the Kings of Judah." Other sources include temple archives and cycles of stories about Elisha, Elijah, and Isaiah. Two principles influenced the Deuteronomic editors. They were the mandatory worship of God in the temple at Jerusalem and the rewarding or punishment of those who obeyed or disobeyed the covenant. There are believed to have been two stages of the Deuteronomic editing of Kings. One editing was to have taken place during the time of Josiah and one after the Exile, about 460 B.C. near the freeing of Jehoiachin. Kings is divided into three sections: the succession and rule of Solomon; the divided kingdoms; and the survival and final collapse of Judah.

First Kings continues where 2 Samuel stops. While Kings and Chronicles deal with the same historical period, each writes from a different point of view. Kings tells of the political and royal life of the nation. Chronicles tells of those events from a priestly and ecclesiastical perspective. The genealogies of 1 Chronicles 1—9 describe the Davidic line, the descendants of Levi and the two tribes of Judah and Benjamin. An outline of 1 Kings follows:

I. *The United Kingdom, 1:1—11:43*
  A. *David, 1:1—2:11*
    1. David makes Solomon king, 1:1-53.
    2. David gives a charge to Solomon, 2:1-9.
    3. David's death, 2:10, 11; see also 1 Chronicles 29:26-30.
  B. *Solomon, 2:12—11:43*
    1. The beginning of Solomon's reign, 2:12—3:28; see 2 Chronicles 2:1-13.
    2. Solomon in all his glory, 4:1—10:29; see 2 Chronicles 1:14-9:28.
II. *The Divided Kingdom, 12:1—22:53*
  A. *The Kingdom of Judah, 12:1-19*
    1. Foolishness of Rehoboam, 12:1-15; see 2 Chronicles 10:1-11.
    2. Rebellion of the ten tribes, 12:16-19; see 2 Chronicles 10:12-19; 11:1-4.
  B. *The Kingdom of Israel, 12:20—14:20*
    1. Sin of Jeroboam, 12:20-33.
    2. God's Interposition, 13:1-32.
    3. Jeroboam's continued sin, 13:33—14:18.
    4. Jeroboam's death, 14:19, 20.
  C. *The Kingdom of Judah, 14:21—15:24*
    1. Judah's sin, 14:21-24; see 2 Chronicles 12:1.
    2. God's correction and forgiveness, 14:25-30; see 2 Chronicles 12:2-12.
    3. Death of Rehoboam, 14:31; see 2 Chronicles 12:13-16.
    4. Abijam, 15:1-8; see 2 Chronicles 13:1-2.
    5. Asa, 15:9-24; see 2 Chronicles 14:1; 16:1-6, 12-14.
  C. *The Kingdom of Israel, 15:25—22:40*
    1. Nadab, 15:25, 26.
    2. Baasha, 15:27-34.
    3. God's message, 16:1-7.
    4. Elah, 16:8-10.
    5. Zimri, 16:11-20.
    6. Omri, 16:21-28.

For homiletical purposes preachers should note that in 1 Kings 1:50 and 2:23 we have the first recorded instances of the horns of the altar as a refuge. In the light of the controversy over the sanctuary movement, some preachers may or may not be led to use these passages as texts since seeking sanctuary at the altar did not save Adonijah from the wrath of Solomon. Abiathar, 2:26-27, Joab, 2:28-35, and Shimei, 2:36-46, were threats to young Solomon's reign and were removed as Solomon's adversaries.

In 1 Kings 5:5 and 8:27 the very first clear theological statement of a spiritual conception of God appears. Solomon's temple was not a house for God to live in as pagan priests and their followers believed. Solomon's temple was constructed for the name of the Lord. Preachers will not want to miss this insight.

2 Kings

The second book of Kings contains the history of Israel and Judah from Ahab to the captivity, a period of about 300 years.

Second Kings informs readers about Elijah, the death of Ahaziah, Elisha, the Jehu dynasty, the time of Athaliah to the demise of Uzziah, the decline of Israel, the threat of Assyria, Josiah and Deuteronomic reform, and the last years of Judah. Ending with a note of hope, 2 Kings informs readers that Nebuchadnezzar's successor, Evil-Merodach, released Jehoiachin from prison and gave him a place above other nobles. The research of archaeological findings corroborates the text in as much as the tablets tell about rations of oil and grain that were paid to Jehoiachin.

Preachers interested in building a series of sermons on 2 Kings could divide the book into the following four broad areas:

1. The Closing Ministry of Elijah.

2. The Ministry of Elisha.
3. The Fall of Israel.
4. The Fall of Judah.

1 and 2 Chronicles

The two books of Chronicles are part of a larger history which includes Ezra and Nehemiah. The similarities in style and vocabulary, the lengthy lists of genealogies, and the large interest in the temple at Jerusalem suggest the commonality of authorship. Ezra resumes exactly where 2 Chronicles stops. Narration in the four books is continuous. The books of Chronicles report the history of the nation from Adam through David and Solomon to the captivity, stopping with Cyrus' release of the Jews from captivity. Ezra and Nehemiah continue the completion of Jewish history by describing the various states of the return of the released Jews to Palestine. The author of Chronicles may have been a priest of the Levites or a singer who was deeply involved in the Jerusalem temple, its functions, personnel, and history. A topical outline of the books is provided:

1 Chronicles
The Lord's People, 1—9.
The Lord's Anointed, 10—12.
The Lord's Ark, 12—16.
The Lord's Covenant, 17—21.
The Lord's Temple, 22—29.
2 Chronicles
The Golden Age of Solomon, 1—9.
The Kings of Judah, 10—26.

In 1 Kings 7:8 the text explains that Solomon built a separate house for Pharaoh's daughter. Second Chronicles 8:11 informs the reader that it was not in Jerusalem because Solomon did not believe that an idolatrous wife should live in the holy city. Kings does not record any noble act of Abijah. But 2 Chronicles 13 records both his devout address and fervent prayer to God. Only 2 Chronicles 16:12 reveals that good King Asa neglected the Lord in his last illness and that good King Jehoshaphat entered into a threefold sinful alliance: matrimonial, (2 Chronicles 21:6); military, (2 Chronicles 18:3); and commercial, (2 Chronicles 20:35). Only 2 Chronicles 24:7 reports that Athaliah committed sacrilege and only 2 Chronicles 26:16-21 reports why the Lord smote Uzziah with leprosy.

The conclusion of 2 Chronicles speaks of the majesty and universalism of God. Those words are memorable:

> Thus says Cyrus king of Persia, "The Lord, the God of heaven, has given me all the kingdoms of the earth, and He has appointed me to build Him a house in Jerusalem, which is in Judah. Whoever there is among you of all His people, may the Lord his God be with him, and let him go up!" (2 Chronicles 36:23, NAS).

Ezra-Nehemiah

Ezra-Nehemiah was originally one book and is a continuation of Chronicles. It tells about the return of some of the exiles after the liberating decree mentioned in 2 Chronicles 36:23. The people liberated had been under the bondage of the Babylonians. Ezra-Nehemiah is the only biblical work of the Persian period, 546-334 B.C. During this period, the Greeks won victories against the Persians—Marathon in 490 B.C. and Thermopylae and Salamis in 480 B.C.

Four stages of return took place from Babylon to Palestine during the same time of the Grecian victories against their enemies. The four stages of the liberation process set in motion by Persian leader Cyrus are:

1. A return under Cyrus in 538 B.C. led by Sheshbazzar with an aborted attempt to rebuild the temple.
2. A return under Darius I (521-485 B.C.) led by Zerrubbabel and Joshua, who completed the temple with the encouragement of the prophets Haggai and Zerubbabel.
3. A return under Artaxerxes led by Nehemiah (464-423

B.C.) who rebuilt the walls of Jerusalem and who, after returning from a trip to Persia, was disappointed to find his reforms neglected.

4. A return under Artaxerxes II (404-388 B.C.) led by Ezra who read to the people the book of the law of Moses.

During building programs, pastors and ministers have found numerous homiletical nuggets in Nehemiah, and pastors who emphasize Bible studies can discover an equal number of sermonic gems from mining texts in both Ezra and Nehemiah. Those who have sought biblical justification against racial intermarriage have often used Nehemiah to promote a sub-Christian ethic that is contrary to the spirit of Jesus and a morality that is antithetical to the morality of Ruth, Jonah, and Esther.

Esther

The book of Esther is read at the feast of Purim in the early spring. The name Purim comes from Pur, or lot, used by Haman to determine the most propitious day for the massacre of the Jews. The story is set in the reign of Xerxes I or Ahasuerus. Scholars argue about the date Esther was written. Perhaps it can be safely dated about the middle of the fourth century. This would explain the use of many Persian words and the knowledge of Persian customs. However, there is strong support for dating Esther near the latter period of the Maccabees when the Jews were ruthlessly treated and dehumanized by their enemies.

The essence of Esther reveals the hostility that existed between Haman, an employee of the king, and Mordecai, a relative of Esther, the queen. Haman hated all Jews, especially Mordecai, who refused to bow and scrape to Haman. But Mordecai learned that two eunuchs were plotting to kill the king. He revealed the plot to Hadassah or Esther, his beautiful young cousin who was now the queen. She told the king. The plotters were killed and the event was recorded in the king's chronicles.

Haman, meanwhile, continued to rise in the kingdom and became increasingly angry that Mordecai, the Benjamite, refused to bow to him. Haman was an Amalekite. Since Moses' day, the Israelites had trouble with the Amalekites, and since Saul's day, the Amalekite king, Agag, had trouble with Benjamite Saul. Haman boiled in anger, perhaps with ancient ancestral memories. Haman persuaded the king to allow him to have permission and power to have the Jews exterminated on the thirteenth day of Adar which falls during March-April. Letters were sent by couriers to all parts of the empire with this ugly announcement.

Mordecai and the Jews tore their clothes. They dressed up in mourning clothes of sackcloth and ashes. Mordecai mourned by the king's gate. Queen Esther, the beautiful cousin of Mordecai who was Jewish incognito, sent clothes to Mordecai. He refused to wear them. He sent her a copy of Haman's decree and begged her to save her people, reminding her that she too would die if the decree was carried out. She could not hide in the king's palace. Esther responded by asking Mordecai to gather all the Jews together and fast while she made the attempt to save her people. She said, "If I perish, I perish."

On the third day Esther took the risk. In her royal robes she entered the inner court. To her relief, the king held out the golden sceptre to her and promised to grant her request, even to the half of his kingdom. She promised to announce her petition at a banquet to which she invited Haman. She put off her announcment at the first banquet and invited Haman and the king to a second banquet.

Meanwhile, Haman arrogantly boasted to his wife and friends of his great rapport with the king and queen. But that night the invisible God, whose name does not even appear in the book of Esther, induced sleeplessness in the king. He had his official chronicles read to him. He heard how Mordecai once saved his life. He gained a God-given desire to show gratitude to Mordecai for his loyalty.

So the king asked, "Who is in the court?" Haman, eager to display his new power by asking for Mordecai's death, was ready to answer the question, "What shall be done unto the man whom the king delighteth to honor?" He incorrectly assumed that he was the man, so he suggested that the man whom the king desired to honor should be dressed in royal robes and ride on the king's horse through the city. The king agreed and named Mordecai as the man he sought to honor. Haman was humiliated in his heart. He led Mordecai throughout the city. His wife and friends warned him that the tide had turned against him. Nonetheless, Haman attended the second banquet.

There Queen Esther made her emotional plea that the king must save her and her people. She fingered Haman as the wicked adversary. The angry king went out into the palace garden to allow his hot temper to cool. But when he returned to find Haman fallen upon the bed where Esther was, he interpreted Haman's act as a sexual attack. However, Haman was attempting a common oriental gesture of crying for mercy as he perhaps seized and kissed Esther's feet. King Ahasuerus then ordered his attendants to cover Haman's face and remove him from the room to be hanged on the gallows that Haman had prepared for Mordecai.

The reversal of injustice was completed when Mordecai was given the signet ring with Haman's position and the power to make a new decree which allowed the Jews to take revenge upon their enemies. At Esther's special request, the ten sons of Haman were killed. This marked the extinction of the Amalekite tribe. The feast of Purim was established as a day for gladness and feasting and for sending to each other choice portions. However, this feast was not one of the feasts listed for observance in the Pentateuch.

Three sermon outlines are illustrated as models for possible biographical preaching from Esther.

    I. *Haman*
       His power.
       His pride.
       His plot.
       His pitiful destiny.
   II. *Mordecai*
       His dignity.

His difficulty.
His deliverance.
His destiny.
III. *Esther*
Her physical beauty.
Her spiritual beauty.
Her dignity shown at last.
Her beautiful example.

These examples are by no means complete. Perhaps they could be used as primers of homiletical thinking in order to provoke the more perfect rendering of exegetical intentionality and integrity in preaching the beautiful narratives of Esther. Esther merits a place of honor among the women of the Bible. Her name can mean a star. Before she became a queen, Esther's name meant myrtle. Just as God used an Eastern Jewish orphan, so can God use persons today who will make themselves available. Esther is an illustrious story of the providence of God. God's name does not need to be called in order for God to be at work. God moves quietly and invisibly in human history. God often travels incognito. He influences history without the awareness of His friends or foes. God is the sovereign Lord of history.

Preaching from the Prophets

A student of philosophy who turns from the discourses of the great metaphysicians to the orations of the prophets may feel as if he were going from the realm of the sublime to an area of trivialities. Instead of dealing with the timeless issues of being and becoming, of matter and form, of definitions and demonstrations, he is thrown into orations about widows and orphans, about the corruption of judges and affairs of the marketplace. Instead of showing us a way through the elegant mansions of the mind, the prophets take us to the slums. Their breathless impatience with injustice may strike us as hysteria. . . . But if such deep insensitivity to evil is to be called hysterical, what name should be given to the abysmal indifference to evil which the prophet bewails? (Abraham Joshua Heschel, as quoted from the foreword of *Tikkun*, Vol. 1, No. 2, 1986.)

After preaching from the law and the historical, poetic, and wisdom literature of the Old Testament, responsible preachers will give serious thought towards mining the treasures of the prophets. Scholarly treatises are voluminous on prophetic literature.

Several terms are used in the Hebrew Bible to define the functions of prophets. The word *ro'eh* means seer. Eleven times "seer" is used in the Old Testament. Samuel was a seer who had the ability to look into the mysterious in order to provide answers about the hidden and the unknown.

Chozeh, which means gazing or seeing, is used twenty-two times in the Hebrew Bible. It places emphasis upon the reception of divine truth and not the proclamation of God's message. Balaam and Gad were among the gazers.

The word *nabhi* is used three hundred times in the Hebrew Bible. This word comes from the Semitic root *naba'*, which means to speak. In Arabic the word means to deliver a message on behalf of one who has commissioned the messenger. Read Exodus 7:1, Deuteronomy 18:18, Jeremiah 1:9, and 15:19 for greater understanding of the idea of sending one to deliver a message. The Greek version of the Old Testament or the Septuagint uses the word prophet. This simply means a forthteller or one who speaks on behalf of another.

First Samuel 10:5 tells about ecstatic prophets who danced, sang, and roamed the countryside in prophetic bands. They interpreted dreams and practiced the proclamation of mystical oracles. They were like soothsayers. Later, individual seers came into power and after them there seem to have been prophets who became court prophets or advisers of kings. First Samuel 9:9, 2 Samuel 7:2, 1 Kings 22:6, and 34:10 illustrate some of these ideas.

Dr. Kyle M. Yates has suggested a chronology of the prophets which appears as follows:

The Early Group

Moses	1447-1400 B.C.	In Egypt and the wilderness
Samuel	1100 B.C.	In Israel
Elijah	870 B.C.	In Israel
Elisha	850 B.C.	In Israel
Joel	835-820 B.C.	In Israel
Jonah	800 B.C.	In Israel

Scholars debate whether this Jonah of circa 800 B.C. is the same Jonah mentioned in the book of Jonah. More on this subject is available in the introduction to the book of Jonah in any of the scholarly commentaries.

The Eighth Century Group

Amos	760 B.C.	In Israel
Hosea	745 B.C.	In Israel
Isaiah	740-698 B.C.	In Jerusalem
Micah	735 B.C.	In Jerusalem

Scholarly discussions on Isaiah can be read in depth in scholarly commentaries or resource materials. Some say there must have been three Isaiahs.

Book	Chapters	
Proto-Isaiah	1—39	Preexilic
Deutero-Isaiah	40—54	Exile
Trito-Isaiah	55—66	Postexilic

The Seventh Century Group

Zephaniah	630-622 B.C.	In Jerusalem
Jeremiah	626-585 B.C.	In Jerusalem and Egypt
Nahum	625-612 B.C.	In Jerusalem
Habakkuk	610-605 B.C.	In Jerusalem

The Exilic Group

| Obadiah | 586 B.C. | In Jerusalem or Babylon |
| Ezekiel | 592 B.C. | In Babylon |

The Postexilic Group

Haggai	520 B.C.	In Jerusalem
Zechariah	520 B.C.	In Jerusalem
Malachi	435 B.C.	In Jerusalem[35]

Preachers who are interested in studying pre-classical prophecy would do well to read T. H. Robinson, *Prophecy and the Prophets in Ancient Israel* (1923), C. Kuhl, *The Prophets of Israel* (1961), and E. W. Wheaton, *Old Testament Prophets*, as well as J. Lindblom, *Prophecy in Ancient Israel* (1962).

The prophetic office was founded during a crisis time of Israel's history. Belief in Yahweh was eroding due to a religious syncretism with the gods of other nations. As Israel formed political alliances with neighboring countries, the belief in Yahweh degenerated. As the tribes of Israel transcended through economic, social, and cultural changes and as they moved from nomadic to rural and from agrarian to town-dwelling (where the land owners in the towns perpetrated economic injustices upon the poor), Yahweh's directives were thrown aside creating an ethical and theological gap which the prophets were called upon to address. The intricacies of world history in the dominating appearances of the Assyrians, Babylonians, and Persians created a climate which the prophets courageously addressed as spokespersons of Yahweh. This meant that the prophets not only knew the old Israel-Covenant tradition of Moses and the Zion-Messianic tradition of David, but also the nuances and contours of world history. The mission of the prophets was not only to Israel but also to the nations. This is clearly seen in the call of Jeremiah:

35. Kyle M. Yates, *Preaching from the Prophets*, (New York: Harper and Brothers Publishing, 1942), pp. 4-5.

Now the word of the Lord came to me saying, Before I formed you in the womb I knew you, and before you were born I consecrated you; I appointed you a prophet to the nations (Jeremiah 1:5, RSV).

Isaiah

In 735 B.C. Isaiah warned his people how Yahweh would enlist other nations as instruments to judge Israel:

In that day the Lord will whistle for the fly which is at the sources of the streams of Egypt, and for the bee which is in the land of Assyria. And they will all come and settle in the steep ravines, and in the clefts of the rocks, and on all thornbushes, and on all the pastures (Isaiah 7:18, 19, RSV).

With irony and humor, Isaiah spoke about God shaving with a hired razor. This would be an interesting text for preaching.

In that day the Lord will shave with a razor which is hired beyond the river—with the Kings of Assyria—the head and hair of the feet, and it will sweep away the beard also (Isaiah 7:20, RSV).

The prophets addressed a message with universal implications to Israel and her neighbors by metaphorical use of irony and humor. But they also used dramatic and shocking symbolic behavior. Ahijah, the Shilonite, tore his garment into twelve pieces and gave them to Jeroboam. (Read 1 Kings 11:29.) Isaiah drew up a tablet with a name on it and walked about naked as if he were a deportee or a prisoner of war. (See Isaiah 8:1-4 and Isaiah 20:1-6.) Jeremiah broke a flask, wore a yoke of wood, and purchased a field just as his nation was being carried into Babylonian captivity. (Read Jeremiah 19:1ff., Jeremiah 27:2ff., and Jeremiah 32:6ff.) Much of Ezekiel's behavior was bizarre and erratic as he undertook radically disturbing means to awaken apathetic Israel to hear the word of the Lord. These incidents can be read in Ezekiel 4 and 5. The symbolic acts of the prophets were intensified forms of prophetic speech.

There was a strangeness about prophetic preaching which gave it a uniqueness distinct from the theology of the prophets' predecessors who interpreted the law and shared theology through oral traditions. The prophets brought a newness of ideas into utterance. Jeremiah spoke of a new covenant, and Isaiah talked about a new Exodus. Hosea gave a word about a new entry into the land, and Ezekiel spoke of a new temple.

The prophets talked about the God who performs a new deed for His people when it appears that they have destroyed themselves. But the prophets understood that the God who gave them the message of new possibilities was the sovereign Lord of all history. This God works when persons believe He is sleeping. This God is not controlled by the natural cycles of the seasons nor by any predetermined historical processes. The cosmology of Near Eastern myths and the determinism of Greek historians were powerless in setting limitations upon Yahweh, the God of the prophets. In Grecian thought, the ages of humankind could and would experience a devolution from a golden age to an iron age to ages inferior until the cycle became an ideal golden one again. But the God of the prophets was not affected by impersonal forces of history. As Isaiah said:

> Behold the nations are as a drop in the bucket, and are accounted as the dust on the scales; behold he takes up the isles like fine dust (Isaiah 40:15, RSV).

The prophets believed in the transcendence of Yahweh who moved in history while being above and in control of history.

> For my thoughts are not your thoughts, neither are your ways my ways, says the Lord. For as the heavens are higher than the earth, so are my ways higher than your ways and my thoughts than your thoughts (Isaiah 55:8, 9, RSV).

There was a certainty that Yahweh, the God of the prophets, was trustworthy. The world is temporal. Persons are transitory. The accountability of God to Himself and the reliability of God to His people constitute a word much more certain than the uncer-

tainty of the stockbrokers who control the economic systems of the
world and the political powerbrokers who view themselves as the
earthshakers and worldmovers.

With poetic beauty and literary elegance Isaiah describes the
immutability of God:

> For as the rain and the snow come down from heaven and
> return not thither but water the earth, making it bring
> forth and sprout, giving seed to the sower, and bread to
> the eater; so shall my word be that goes forth from my
> mouth, it shall not return unto me empty, but it shall ac-
> complish that which I purpose, and prosper in the thing
> for which I sent it (Isaiah 40:10, 11, RSV).

Habakkuk

It has not been easy for prophets to accept the truth about
both the greatness and goodness of God. If God is good, why do
the wicked prosper while the good suffer? Does God's word ac-
complish the purpose for which God has sent it? Is God great
enough to insure the visibility of goodness in society. Is God active
in the world on behalf of His elect? These questions were the questions of Habakkuk.

> The oracle of God which Habakkuk the prophet saw. "O
> Lord, how long shall I cry for help, and thou wilt not
> hear? Or cry to thee Violence! and thou wilt not save?"
> (Habakkuk 1:1, RSV).

In response to the frustrated, passionate protest of the prophet
comes the unapologetic answer of God.

> "Look among the nations and see; wonder and be as-
> tounded. For I am doing a work in your days that you
> would not believe it told. For lo, I am rousing the Chal-
> deans, that bitter and hasty nation, who march through
> the breadth of the earth to seize habitations not their
> own" (Habakkuk 1:5, 6, RSV).

The prophet is not happy with God's answer. He does not accept God's thesis. He debates with God. He complains about the moral indifference of God. He attempts to show God how illogical and injurious and non-Godlike He is.

"Thou who art of purer eyes than to behold evil and canst not look on wrong, why dost thou look on faithless men, and art silent when the wicked swallows up the man more righteous than he?" (Habakkuk 1:13, RSV).

After expressing his unhappiness to God, Habakkuk refuses to disavow his faith in God but expresses a determination to live with unanswered questions while waiting for God to answer his complaint. He says:

"I will take my stand to watch, and station myself on the tower, and look forth to see what he will say to me, and what I will answer concerning my complaint" (Habakkuk 2:1, RSV).

God answers Habakkuk with information that describes the self-destructive nature of evil. This reality informs the prophet that evil runs its course. There is a basic need to be patient while evil is in the process of its self-destruction.

"For the vision awaits its time; it hastens to the end—it will not lie. If it seems slow, wait for it; it will surely come, it will not delay. Behold, he whose soul is not upright in him shall fail, but *the righteous shall live by his faith.* Moreover, wine is treacherous; the arrogant man shall not abide. His greed is as wide as Sheol; like death he has never enough" (Habakkuk 2:3-5a, RSV).

The peak of the mountain of faith is climbed and the triumph of faith over the mystery of the power of evil in the presence of the powerlessness of good are gifts of God's saving grace as the prophet poetically proclaims:

"Though the fig trees do not blossom, nor fruit be on the vines, the produce of the olive fail and the fields yield no

food, the flock be cut off from the fold and there be no
herd in the stalls, yet I will rejoice in the Lord, I will joy in
the God of my salvation. God, the Lord is my strength; he
makes my feet like hinds feet, he makes me tread upon my
high places" (Habakkuk 3:17-19, RSV).

Nahum

The theme articulated in Habakkuk has continuing relevance
in the preaching of Nahum, who lived and preached between the
fall of Thebes in 663 B.C. and the fall of Nineveh in 612 B.C.

Nimrod was the founder of Nineveh. From her birth, Nineveh
arose to maturity as an ancient queen among her sister cities. With
walls one hundred feet high, seven and one half miles in cir-
cumference and wide enough for three chariots to drive abreast,
Nineveh was a mighty mistress among the maiden urban centers of
the ancient world. Nineveh had twelve hundred defense towers
and a moat outside the walls over one hundred and forty feet wide
and sixty feet deep. Such security made Nineveh almost inde-
structible.

Because of the extreme cruelty of Nineveh, Nahum had intense hatred for the Assyrians. His strong language against them is
a passionate invective of a prophet with a deep sense of justice.

Nineveh is like a pool whose waters run away. Halt, Halt,
they cry; but none turn back. Plunder the silver. Plunder
the gold! There is no end of treasure or wealth of every
precious thing. . . . Behold I am against you says the Lord
of hosts, and I will burn your chariots in smoke. . ."
(Nahum 2:8, 9, 13a, RSV).

In 626 B.C., Nabopolassar became the king of the Babylonians. For four years Nineveh fought the Babylonians for survival.
The Medes and Scythians joined forces with Babylon, and complete was Nineveh's fall. The city fell in 612 B.C. never to
dominate the world again.

Zephaniah

In Zephaniah there is a beautiful balance between the judg-

ment and mercy of God. The prophet introduces the book by condemning idol worship. He announces the fearful, terrible day of
the Lord.

> The great day of the Lord is near, near and hastening fast,
> the sound of the day of the Lord is bitter, the mighty man
> cries aloud there. A day of wrath is that day, a day of
> distress and anguish, a day of ruin and devastation, a day
> of darkness and gloom, a day of clouds and darkness, a
> day of trumpet blast and battle cry against the fortified
> cities and against the lofty battlements (Zephaniah
> 1:14-16, RSV).

After condemning Philistia, Moab, Ammon, Ethiopia, and
Assyria in chapter 2:4-15, the prophet Zephaniah, in chapter 3:1-7,
condemns Jerusalem for her faithless living. The mercy and com-
passion of God balances the prophetic message of chapter 3:8-20.
Some observations might be made by preachers who read Zephaniah with an inquiring mind. The book opens by saying, "The
word of the Lord which came to Zephaniah, the son of
Cushi. . . ." Why do Bible scholars overlook the term "Cushi"? Do
they have fears that a powerful Black man could have been the
father of Zephaniah? Chapter 3:10 says:

> From beyond the rivers of Ethiopia my suppliants, the
> daughter of my dispersed one shall bring offering.

Why is Zephaniah concerned about Ethiopia? Why didn't he
neglect the mentioning of Ethiopia as is often done by contemporary historians who, in the 20th century, write as if there is no
positive and productive Black presence enriching human life? Why
do so many renown biblical scholars explain away Black presence
in the Scriptures? In doing this many arguments are used. Professor
Randall Bailey, professor of Old Testament at Interdenomina-
tional Theological Center in Atlanta, Georgia, has discussed this
issue with the author of this manuscript. Dr. Charles Copher,
retired dean and professor of Old Testament at I.T.C., first introduced to the author that "Cushi" was the Black one, as he
shared in a course he taught at the Graduate Theological Union in

Berkeley, California. Nevertheless, the balanced message of Zephaniah which emphasizes retribution and redemption based on repentance is the cardinal principle for the homiletical development of Zephaniah.

Obadiah

The continuation of the theme of Habakkuk and Zephaniah is carried over in Obadiah, the shortest of the Old Testament books.

The prophecy of Obadiah is directed at Esau's descendants who moved into a locale south of the Dead Sea. This place was called Edom and was one hundred miles long and fifty miles wide. The Edomites made raids on neighboring tribes and traveling merchants. They would then retreat to Sela (Petra), Teman, and Bozrah, which were highly fortified. One of the wonders of the world, with cliffs more than seven hundred feet high that gave shelter to a narrow ravine of one mile in length, Petra was an impossible place to destroy. Persons who visit the Holy Land still visit Petra.

The problem with the Edomites was further complicated because they refused to allow the Israelites passage through their territory at the time of the Exodus. In the struggle for the conquest of Palestine, the Edomites fought against Israel. David subdued the land and Solomon continued to hold it in subjection. In the time of Ahaz, the Edomites rebelled. When Nebuchadnezzar came against Judah in 587 B.C., we do not know how the Edomites fared. Judas Maccabaeus drove them out of southern Judah in 164 B.C. John Hyrcanus later compelled them to accept Judaism. They became the hated Idumeans that gave to the Jews the Herodian family. The Idumeans disappeared from history in A.D. 70 at the time of the destruction of Jerusalem.

An outline of Obadiah is as follows:

    I. Edom shall perish.
    II. The cause.
    III. Judgment.
    IV. Judah shall be restored.

Obadiah includes a most moving and passionate passage of this prophet:

> Behold, I will make you small among the nations; you are greatly despised. The arrogance of your heart has deceived you, you who live in the clefts of the rock, in the loftiness of your dwelling place, who say in your heart, who will bring me down to earth? Though you build high like the eagle, though you set your nest among the stars, from there I will bring you down, declares the Lord. If thieves came to you, if robbers by night—O how you will be ruined!—Would they not steal only until they had enough? (Obadiah 1:2-5, NAS).

Obadiah believed in the justice of God. He saw God as being in control of the universe. He believed that nations reaped what they sowed. He spoke of the Day of the Lord as the time of God's judgment upon Edom and all nations.

> For the day of the Lord draws near on all the nations. As you have done, it will be done to you. Your dealings will return on your own head. Because just as you drank on My holy mountain, all the nations will drink continually. They will drink and swallow, and become as if they had never existed (Obadiah 1:15, 16, NAS).

Jonah

Jonah, the son of Amittai, is mentioned in 2 Kings 14:25. He lived during the time of Jeroboam II. Not much is known about him. However, the book of Jonah is about Jonah himself rather than a collection of Jonah's messages. The book is dated after the exile, possibly in the fifth century. The universality of God's concern for all nations is stressed in direct contrast with the Jewish nationalism of postexilic times.

Three interpretations have been given of the book of Jonah. There is the mythological or parabolic interpretation which sees Jonah as an imaginary character with an imaginary experience.

The allegorical interpretation considers Jonah to be a human type of the nation of Israel. The fish is a type of Israel's captivity. The historical interpretation, in keeping with the author of Tobit, the author of Third Maccabees, and Josephus, presents Jonah and the facts of the narrative as being literally true.

An outline of Jonah follows:

Chapter 1—Disobedience or running from God.
Chapter 2—Prayer or running to God.
Chapter 3—Preaching or running with God.
Chapter 4—Complaints or running ahead of God.

A thematic contrast between Deutero-Isaiah and Jonah views the former stressing the nature of Israel's mission and the latter illustrating the form of Israel's mission.

The homiletical thread of Jonah allows preachers to preach about a God who would have His people to love even their enemies as God loves them. The social ethics of Jonah are in sharp contrast to the social ethics of Psalm 137, which has been called an imprecatory psalm.

Haggai

Apparently lacking the spaciousness of mind and the graciousness of heart of Jonah, Amos, Isaiah, and Jeremiah, Haggai was consumed by a single purpose which was to inspire Jewish exiles from Babylon to rebuild the temple. Because Zerubbabel, the temporal ruler, and Joshua, the high priest, were fruitless in influencing the people to rebuild the temple, the prophet Haggai stood with Zechariah in leading the people to rebuild the temple. He used four brief oracles to challenge the people. Haggai 1:2-11 was a word of rebuke and a call to action. Haggai 2:1-9 was a call to courage and encouragement in a time of discouragement. Haggai 2:10-19 called for patience and consecration. Haggai 2:20-23 gave a message of hope and a genuine assurance of the protection of God upon Zerrubbabel.

"On that day," declares the Lord of hosts, "I will take you, Zerubbabel son of Shealtiel, my servant," declares the

Lord, "and I will make you like a signet ring, for I have chosen you," declares the Lord of hosts (Haggai 2:23, NAS).

Zechariah

In those terrible times between 520 B.C. and 516 B.C., Zechariah worked along with Haggai to keep the Jewish people motivated to rebuild the temple. Chapters 1—6 were presented in the forms of visions to challenge the builders in their work. Chapters 7—8 spoke out against formalism and called for practical, ethical behavior. Chapters 9—14 gave disclosures of divine destiny and utilized messianic themes. The priestly and the kingly offices were united in the Branch. In the New Testament, the gospel writers quoted from chapter 9:9-10 to describe the entry of Christ into Jerusalem on Palm Sunday.

Because of the sharp contrasts between chapters 1—8 and 9—14, the scholars believe that these two sections were composed by two different authors. In chapters 1—8, the author speaks in the first person. In chapters 9—14, the author's name is never used. The second section is apocalyptic. The writer of the oracle in 12:1—13:9 expects that when the heathen nations rise to destroy God's people, God will come to their defense, but only one third of the nation will survive as a faithful remnant. In chapter 14 another writer says that after the city has been ravaged and half the population exiled, God in person will appear on the Mount of Olives, which will split in half while the whole land becomes a plain. If the surviving nations fail to worship the Lord and observe the Feast of the Tabernacles, they will be afflicted with droughts.

Malachi

Malachi means my messenger. Malachi wrote at a time when both priests and people were depressed and discouraged by the life they experienced after the return to Judah. They had come with high hopes but were forced to face many disappointments. Where were the blessings that had been promised in Second Isaiah? Where was the God of justice?

The prophet explained that the downfall of Edom was one way God demonstrated His love for them. The breakdown of family life and the sacrificing of imperfect animals by the priests were also reasons for their sad plight. However, the day would come when evildoers would be destroyed and the sun of righteousness would appear with healing in His wings. Elijah, the prophet, would return to turn the hearts of the fathers and children towards each other.

CHAPTER FIVE

Interpreting the Texts of the Old Testament

In April of 1986, Pastor H. N. Edwards of Oxnard, California, and I visited a Baptist Church in Los Angeles, California, to attend the funeral service of a respected and beloved Christian woman. The pastor was gracious and compassionate. His message was comforting and challenging. His delivery was excellent. The audience received the messenger and the message with warmth. The evangelistic appeal of the message was tastefully presented in a context of mourning the loss of a loved one. However, Pastor Edwards and I lamented the fact that the pastor announced as his text the beautiful latter portion of the eighth chapter of Romans and then proceeded to ignore the text. He wooed our intellectual appetites so that we eagerly awaited the insights on the text. But we left the service not knowing any more about Romans than we did when we arrived.

Perhaps he is not all to blame for failing to use biblical exegesis and exegetical theology in preaching. The school which trained the preacher may have failed to instruct him in the art of analyzing the text. Maybe the pressure of parish duties took higher priority over serious, exegetical study and diligent sermon preparation.

Does the average church congregation know when the preacher has given a proper interpretation and application of a sermon text in a preaching situation? Do delivery and style take central place in the preference of those who hear sermons, or do they expect to learn about the meaning of the sermon text? The professionalism of the preacher should influence the degree of cautiousness and care that is exercised in exegeting the sermon text and should determine the quality of preparation which is given to the overall preaching responsibility. Biblical exegesis is difficult, and its practice often escapes mastery. But biblical exegetes are students of a discipline which demands a continuing pursuit of excellence much like the athlete who toils daily in conditioning for his or her "personal best" in skillful performance.

The study of interpreting the biblical text has a long history of debate and discussion. William Ames, who taught at Harvard in the seventeenth century, said that there is only one meaning for every Scripture. He believed that if a text had more than one meaning, then the text would be unclear and the interpreter could not be sure of the intentionality of the text.[36] Building upon Ames' thesis was the view of J. A. Ernesti who saw exegesis as "the discovery of the use of words, the historical circumstances controlling their usage, and the intention of the author who wrote the words of the text."[37]

The debate with J. A. Ernesti during the eighteenth century was promoted by J. S. Semler who rejected "certain supernatural features of the first century A.D."[38]

Friedrich Schleiermacher could not accept the idea that a text should have only one meaning. He taught that "the process of grammatical understanding of an author's words must be distinct and separate from the psychological or technical interpretation. Grammatical interpretation focuses only on the objective side of

36. Walter C. Kaiser, Jr., *Toward an Exegetical Theology: Biblical Exegesis for Preaching and Teaching*, (Grand Rapids, MI: Baker Book House, 1981), p. 24.
37. Op. cit., p. 24.
38. Op. cit., p. 27.

interpretation while the technical deals with the subjective."[39] Scholars who extended the tradition of Schleiermacher include Wilhelm Dilthey (1883-1911), Martin Heidegger (1889-1976), and Rudolph Bultmann (1884-1976). Hans Georg Gadamer (b. 1900) has called this tradition the "New Hermeneutic," and fuses the original outlook of the text with the interpreter's own view of the text.[40]

Meanwhile, Gerhard Ebeling and Ernst Fuchs push the idea that it is not possible for the interpreter of the text to possess objective historical knowledge. The interpreter must live in a psychological sea of relativity. Professor E. D. Hirsch of the University of Virginia brings some sanity to the exegetical crisis. He teaches that the interpreter of the text must make a distinction between meaning and significance. Meaning is that which is represented by a text, its grammar, and the intentions of the author of the text. Meaning is unchanging. But significance is the relationship between the meaning of the text and the idea, time, and situation of the interpreter. Meaning is constant. But significance changes with the changing world of the interpreter.[41]

Biblical scholar Martin Noth in 1952 wrote a book called *The Representation of the Old Testament in Proclamation*. It has been translated from the German language by Professor James Luther Mays and published in a work edited by Professors Claus Westermann and James Luther Mays called *Essays on Old Testament Hermeneutics*. These essays were published in 1963 by John Knox Publishers of Richmond, Virginia. The point made by Professor Noth was that the historical distance between the first hearers of a biblical text and the contemporary hearers or interpreters can be bridged if the past history can be preached as contemporary happenings which call for a contemporaneous love response to God.[42]

The job of biblical interpretation is exactness of interpretation.

39. Op. cit., p. 29.
40. Op. cit., p. 29.
41. Op. cit., p. 32.
42. Op. cit., p. 39.

Any action with less than integrity in interpretation is eisegesis, which results when the feelings and cultural biases of the exegete distort the true meaning of the biblical text. In an attempt to avoid these excesses, the serious-minded should strive to master *textual* analysis, *literary* analysis, *historical* analysis, and *theological* analysis. If the serious-minded cannot read the sermon text in the biblical languages, it would be most helpful if careful study could be made of such modern translations as the *Revised Standard Version*, the *New English Bible*, the *New American Standard Bible*, the *New International Version* and the *Jerusalem Bible*. If major differences are found in the translations, they should be noted and carefully examined with the aid of exegetical commentaries.

The literary forms used by biblical writers should be a matter of serious study. The forms of biblical literature are prose, poetry, narrative, wisdom, and apocalyptic. Prose may be descriptive, explanatory, emotive or argumentative. The prosaic literature of the Bible is found in history, sermons, addresses, covenants, laws, ritual observances, and prayers. Poetry in the Bible has parallel lines that are often repeated into couplets or triads and sometimes with antithetical lines. Hebrew poets enjoyed paronomasia or the use of puns. Their writings are musical in sound and rhythm. Details on exegesis of poetry can be found in Old Testament introductions.

Historical writings are a form of prose writings. Care should be taken in separating historical reporting from editorial comments and from theological applications that are used for preaching material. The many different ways that the same event has been cited by biblical writers should be noted along with the specific manner in which the material is used in the context offered by the exegete. Contextual study should visualize the paragraph, chapter, and book contents in light of the canonical context of the Bible as it is also presented in its contemporary context. To do less is to torture a text or Scripture passage out of its social location into the orphan status of proof texting.

Wisdom writings can either be of a philosophical nature, an extended form of developing a point of view in an attempt to adequately discuss a life issue, or a collection of short, pithy statements, as in Proverbs. The last literary form is apocalyptic in that it uses rich symbolism that involves animals, angels, demons, and persons to paint a word picture of the future. Mysticism, visions, and dreams as well as numbers that are sometimes used with geometrical progression constitute the world of the apocalyptic. Many of the metaphors of the past are projected into the future in apocalyptic literature.

Theological word books, theological dictionaries, and books on biblical semantics as well as theological and linguistic lexicons are necessary tools for all who would practice the art of proclamation. Old Testament concordances and biblical atlases are indispensable tools for perfecting the practice of proclamation.

Finally, the practice of the presence of God is important for all persons who dare to speak for God. The pressure of parish duties, the near, desperate cry of the community for leadership in the civic arena, and ecclesiastical politics can insidiously erode the priority of precious moments in the presence of God. To their surprise and dismay, powerful practitioners of proclamation can easily become Samsons diminished into spiritual pygmies.

> And she said, "The Philistines are upon you, Samson!"
> And he awoke from his sleep and said, "I will go out as at
> other times and shake myself free." But he did not know
> that the Lord had departed from him (Judges 16:20,
> NASB).

The practice of proclamation is a joyous adventure of service and inner fulfillment for those who will do justice, love kindness, and walk humbly with God (Micah 6:8).

In addition to the challenge of Micah to develop a rich devotional life, there is the need to cultivate intellectual curiosity and creative imagination for effective preaching. An unceasing commitment must be made to continuing education and inventive reflection upon the material studied. Hence, private time should not only be set aside for communication with God, but time should also be preserved for individual study and successive moments for a theological, musical, or poetic improvisation upon the thematic content that constitutes the continuing education curriculum.

Source materials are necessary for thoughtful preaching. In addition to biblical tools that aid correct exegesis of the biblical text, I have been helped by reading *Quarterly Review*, a scholarly journal for reflection on ministry. This magazine is a publication of the United Methodist Church. Scholars from Candler, Emory, Yale, Claremont, Duke, Vanderbilt, and Southern Methodist Universities and Divinity Schools write for *Quarterly Review*. These persons speak to me from a liberal perspective and knock me out of my dogmatic slumbers. Another most helpful journal of Bible and theology is *Interpretation*, published by Union Theological Seminary in Richmond, Virginia. Voices from Union Theological Seminary in New York City and Andover Newton Theological Center in Boston aid me in keeping abreast of the latest in scholarship. *Interpretation* also includes articles by some European scholars.

I also read *Theology Today*, an important quarterly published by Princeton University. (Although this journal has many Presbyterian scholars on its advisory board, a balance in reading results due to my reading the *Quarterly Review*, which comes from the Armenian tradition and *Theology Today*, which comes from the Calvinistic tradition.) A very excellent proclamation and exegetical basis comes from the respected and revered *Review and Expositor*, a Baptist journal sophisticated and second to none. Published by Southern Baptists, I have found that this journal from the Southern Baptist Seminary in Louisville is classic and ecumenical and defies each and every commonly known stereotype of Southern Baptists.

My own tradition in the Black church has made it necessary for me to drink from the fountain of ecumenical Black scholars who developed the *International Denominational Center Journal of I.T.C.* in Atlanta, Georgia. A continuing communication with I.T.C. has enabled me to remain not an authority, but an ever-growing student of parish ministry and classic biblical scholarship.

Since the Allen Temple Baptist Church is serving the Bay Area, I have not hesitated to study under the most brilliant of American Baptists who teach at the American Baptist Seminary of the West and the Graduate Theological Union in Berkeley, California. (Pastors shortchange themselves when they ignore rich and ripe scholarship in their own geographical communities.) It is also important that pastors read the papers, studies, and books published and endorsed by the Academy of Homiletics.

My own growth has been inspired by advice given me by the famous Dr. James Forbes of Union Theological Seminary of New York. He has advised me to have a preaching coach. Dr. Forbes is considered an authority on preaching. Yet he has a preaching coach at times. Persons who serve as my mentors in preaching are Drs. C. A. W. Clark of Dallas, Texas, Gardner C. Taylor of Brooklyn, New York, Henry C. Gregory of Washington, D.C., Charles Adams of Detroit, Michigan, E. K. Bailey of Dallas, Texas, Joel Gregory of Fort Worth, Texas, Harry Wright, William Augustus Jones, and Johnny Youngblood of Brooklyn, New York, Nelson Smith of Birmingham, Alabama, and Fleetwood Irving of Vallejo, California. However, I am deeply indebted to Dr. Edwina Hunter of Pacific School of Religion who works consistently with me to help me not only practice correct exegesis, but also to articulate correctly and to develop my poetic and natural gift in preaching with persuasion and freedom. Pastors should not only look to mentors who are role models, but also should accept constructive criticism and affirmation from skilled teachers and practitioners of the art and science of preaching who dearly love them.

As a Christian pastor who loves the Old Testament, I cannot help but read the Old Testament in the light of New Testament Scriptures. Therefore, my personal theology makes a comparative relationship between the Old and New Testaments. Scholars may deprecate and depreciate my personal theology, nonetheless, I unequivocally affirm my evangelical Christological declaration. In the Old Testament the Word was with God. In the New Testament the Word became flesh. In the Old Testament the law came by Moses. Grace and truth came by Jesus Christ. In the Old Testament, God's law was written on tablets of stone. In the New Testament, God's message was written in human hearts. Christ is the sacrificial Lamb and the loving Shepherd. He is the Water of Life and the Manna from Heaven. He is the Alpha and the Omega, the Resurrection and the Life. He is the Lion of the tribe of Judah. He is the Rose of Sharon and the Lily of the Valley. He is God with us, and for us, and in us. He is the Life, the Truth, and the Way. He is our Saviour and our Lord. He is our Shiloh and our Ebenezer. With love and with joy, I practice the proclamation of God's sacred Word. Like Moses, I wish that all the Lord's people would preach and that the Lord would put His Spirit upon them.[43] May all who do preach and love Jesus Christ become proficient in the practice of the proclamation of God's Living Word!

43. See Numbers 11:24-29.

Bibliography

Achtemeier, Elizabeth. "Deuteronomy, Jeremiah." *Proclamation Commentaries*. Edited by Foster McCurley. Philadelphia: Fortress, 1978.

Alexander, David and Pat. *Eerdmans Concise Bible Handbook*. Grand Rapids: Eerdmans, 1980.

Allerman, H. D. and E. E. Flack, eds. *Old Testament Commentary*. Philadelphia: The Mulenberg Press, 1954.

Alter, Robert. *The Art of Biblical Narrative*. New York: Basic Books, Inc., 1981.

Anderson, Bernhard W. *Out of the Depths: The Psalms Speak for Us Today*. Philadelphia: Westminster, 1983.

Anderson, Ray S. *On Being Human: Essay in Theological Anthropology*. Grand Rapids: Eerdmans, 1982.

Benn, J. Solomon, III, compiler. *Preaching in Ebony*. Grand Rapids: Baker Book House, 1981.

Bible Review. Vol. I, No. 4 (Winter, 1985).

Bible Review. Vol. II, No. 1 (Spring, 1986).

Blackburn, Ruth H. *The Old Testament as Living Literature*. New York: Simon & Schuster, 1964.

Blackwood, Andrew W. *Biographical Teaching for Today*. New York: Simon & Schuster, 1954.

_____. *Preaching from Samuel*. New York: Abingdon, 1946.

Boesak, Allen. *The Finger of God: Sermons on Faith and Socio-Political Responsibility*. Translated from the Afrikaans by Peter Randall. New York: Mary Knoll, Orbis Books, 1979.

Bonhoeffer, Dietrich. *Creation and Fall/Temptation: Two Biblical Studies*. "Creation and Fall," translated by John C. Fletcher. "Temptation," edited by Eberhard Bethge and English translation by Kathleen Downham. New York: MacMillan, 1966.

Bruce, F. F. *The New Testament Development of Old Testament Themes*. Grand Rapids: Eerdmans, 1968.

Brueggemann, Walter. *The Prophetic Imagination*. Philadelphia: Fortress, 1978.

Brueggemann, Walter and Hans Walter Wolff. *The Vitality of Old Testament Tradition*. 2nd edition. Atlanta: John Knox Press, 1982.

Budge, E. A. Wallis. *The Egyptian Book of the Dead: (The Papyrus of Ani) Egyptian Text Transliteration and Translation*. New York: Dover, 1967.

Bullinger, E. W. *Number in Scripture: Its Supernatural Design and Spiritual Significance*. Grand Rapids: Kregel, 1985.

Cate, Robert L. *Old Testament Roots for New Testament Faith*. Nashville: Broadman, 1982.

_____. *These Sought a Country: A History of Israel in Old Testament Times*. Nashville: Broadman Press, 1985.

Charpentier, Etienne. *How to Read the Old Testament*. Translated by John Bowden. New York: Crossroads, 1982.

Coats, George W. "Genesis: With an Introduction to Narrative Literature." *The Forms of the Old Testament Literature*. Vol. I. Edited by Rolf Knierimand and Gene M. Tucker. Grand Rapids: Eerdmans, 1983.

Conner, Kevin J. *The Tabernacle of Moses*. Portland: Bible Press, 1975.

Corcos, Georgette, Rachel Gilon, Yael Lotan, and Marquis Galen, eds. *The Glory of the Old Testament*. Hong Kong: Mandarin Offset, 1984.

Dyrness, William A. *Let the Earth Rejoice: A Biblical Theology of Holistic Mission*. Westchester: Crossway Books, 1983.

Finegan, Jack. *Light from the Ancient Past: The Archeological Background of Hebrew-Christian Religion.* Vol. I. Princeton: Princeton University Press, 1974.

Fishbane, Michael. *Text and Texture: Close Readings of Selected Biblical Texts.* New York: Schocken, 1979.

Fuller, Reginald. *The Use of the Bible in Preaching.* Philadelphia: Fortress, 1981.

Garvie, Alfred E. *A Guide to Preachers.* New York: George H. Doran, 1906.

Girdlestone, Robert B. *Synonyms of the Old Testament.* Grand Rapids: Eerdmans, 1981.

Goldingay, John. "Approaches to Old Testament Interpretation." *Issues in Contemporary Theology.* Edited by I. Howard Marshal. Downers Grove: Intervarsity Press, 1981.

Gollwitzer, Helmut. *Song of Love: A Biblical Understanding of Sex.* Translated by Keith Crim. Philadelphia: Fortress Press, 1979.

Gottwald, Norman K. *The Hebrew Bible: A Socio-Literary Introduction.* Fortress: Philadelphia, 1985.

Gowan, Donald E. *Reclaiming the Old Testament for the Christian Pulpit.* Atlanta: John Knox Press, 1968.

Graves, Robert and Raphael Patai. *Hebrews Myths: The Book of Genesis.* New York: McGraw-Hill, 1966.

Habershon, Ada R. *Hidden Pictures in the Old Testament.* Grand Rapids: Kregel, 1982. Originally published as *Hidden Pictures in the Old Testament, or How the New Testament is Concealed in the Old Testament.* London: Oliphants, 1916.

Haldeman, I. M. *Bible Expositions.* Vol. I. Grand Rapids: Baker, 1964.

Harris, R. Laird, Gleason L. Archer, Jr., and Bruce K. Waltke. *Theological Wordbook of the Old Testament.* Vol. I. Chicago: Moody, 1980.

Harrison, R. K. *The Archaeology of the Old Testament.* New York: Harper & Row, 1963.

Interpretation. Vol. XL, No. 1 (January, 1966).

Jensen, Irving L. *Jensen's Survey of the Old Testament.* Chicago: Moody, 1978.

_____. *Minor Prophets of Israel.* Chicago: Moody, 1975.

Kac, Arthur W. *The Messianic Hope.* Grand Rapids: Baker, 1975.

Kaiser, Walter C., Jr. *A Biblical Approach to Personal Suffering.* Chicago: Moody, 1982.

_____. *The Old Testament in Contemporary Preaching.* Grand Rapids: Baker, 1973.

_____. *Toward an Exegetical Theology: Biblical Exegesis for Preaching and Teaching.* Grand Rapids: Baker, 1981.

_____. *Toward an Old Testament Theology.* Grand Rapids: Zondervan, 1978.

_____. *The Uses of the Old Testament.* Chicago: Moody, 1985.

Kean, Charles Duell. *God's Word to His People.* Philadelphia: Westminster, 1956.

Keller, Werner. *The Bible a History.* 2nd ed. Revised by Joachim Rehork. Translated from German by William Neil and R. H. Rasmussen. Toronto: Bantam, 1981.

Kelly, Balmer H. and Donald G. Miller, eds. *Tools for Bible Study.* Richmond: John Knox, 1957.

Klein, Ralph W. *Israel in Exile.* Philadelphia: Fortress, 1979.

Knight, George A. I. *Deutero-Isaiah: A Theological Commentary on Isaiah 40-55.* New York: Abingdon, 1965.

_____. "Leviticus." *The Daily Study Bible Series.* John C. L. Gibson, General Editor. Philadelphia: Westminster, 1981.

LaSor, William S., David A. Hubbard, and Frederic W. Bush. *Old Testament Survey: The Message, Form and Background of the Old Testament.* Grand Rapids: Eerdmans, 1982.

Lee, Robert G. *Whirlwinds of Gods.* Grand Rapids: Zondervan, 1932.

Limburg, James. *Old Stories for a New Time.* Atlanta: John Knox Press, 1983.

Long, Burke O. *Images of Man and God: Old Testament Short Stories in Literary Focus.* Edited by David M. Gunn. Sheffield, England: Almond Press, 1981.

McCurley, Foster R. "Genesis, Exodus, Leviticus, Numbers." *Proclamation Commentaries.* Edited by Foster R. McCurley. Philadelphia: Fortress, 1979.

_____. *Proclaiming the Promise.* Philadelphia: Fortress, 1974.

McKenzie, John L. *A Theology of Old Testament*. Garden City: Image Books, 1976.

Malcomson, William L., ed. *How to Survive in the Ministry*. Valley Forge: Judson, 1982.

Mears, Henrietta C. *A Look at the Old Testament*. Glendale: G/L Regal Books, 1974.

Montgomery, Felix and Marjory Goldfinch Ward. *God's People: From One to a Nation*. Nashville: Convention Press, 1973.

Napier, Davie. *Word of God, Word of Earth*. Philadelphia: United Church Press, 1976.

Owens, Milton E., Jr. *Outstanding Black Sermons*. Vol. 3. Valley Forge: Judson, 1982.

Payne, David F. "Deuteronomy." *The Daily Study Bible Series*. John C. L. Gibson, General Editor. Philadelphia: Westminster, 1985.

_____. "I & II Samuel." *The Daily Study Bible Series*. John C. L. Gibson, General Editor. Philadelphia: Westminster, 1982.

Penn-Lewis, Jessie. *The Story of Job: A Glimpse into the Mystery of Suffering*. England: The Overcomer Literature Trust, 1902.

Pfeiffer, Charles F. *The Human Side of the Saints*. Grand Rapids: Baker, 1979.

Phillips, John. *100 Sermon Outlines from the Old Testament*. Chicago: Moody, 1979.

Philpot, William M., ed. *Best Black Sermons*. Valley Forge: Judson, 1972.

Rast, Walter E. "Joshua, Judges, Samuel, Kings." *Proclamation Commentaries*. Edited by Foster R. McCurley. Philadelphia: Fortress, 1978.

Ray, Sandy F. *Journeying through a Jungle*. Nashville: Broadman, 1979.

Review and Expositor. "Psalms," Vol. LXXXI, No. 3 (Summer, 1984).

Review and Expositor. "The Revival of Apocalyptic," Vol. LXXII, No. 3 (Summer, 1975).

Review and Expositor. "Old Testament Theology," Vol. LXXIV, No. 3 (Summer, 1977).

Richards, Larry. "Let Day Begin." *Larry Richards Bible Alive Series*.

Elgin: David C. Cook Publishing Company, 1980.

Routley, Erik. *Exploring the Psalms*. Philadelphia: Westminster, 1975.

Ryken, Leland. *How to Read the Bible as Literature*. Grand Rapids: Zondervan, 1984.

Sanders, James A. *Canon and Community*. Edited by Gene M. Tucker. Philadelphia: Fortress, 1984.

_____. *God Has a Story Too*. Philadelphia: Fortress Press, 1980.

_____. *Torah & Canon*. Philadelphia: Fortress, 1972.

Schofield, J. N. *Introducing Old Testament Theology*. Philadelphia: Westminster, 1964.

Shannon, David T. *The Old Testament Experience of Faith*. Valley Forge: Judson Press, 1977.

Smith, J. Alfred., ed. *Outstanding Black Sermons*. Vol. I. Valley Forge: Judson, 1976.

_____. *Preach On!* Nashville: Broadman, 1984.

Smitty, William H. *300 Sermon Outlines from the Old Testament*. Nashville: Broadman, 1982.

Snaith, Norman H. *The Distinctive Ideas of the Old Testament*. London: Epworth, 1983.

Stevenson, Dwight E. *In the Biblical Preacher's Workshop*. Nashville: Abingdon. 1967.

Stewart, Warren H. *Interpreting God's Word in Black Preaching*. Valley Forge: Judson, 1984.

Stuart, Douglas. *Old Testament Exegesis*. 2nd ed. Philadelphia: Westminster, 1984.

Taylor, Gardner C. *The Scarlet Thread*. Elgin: Progressive Baptist Publishing House, 1981.

Terrien, Samuel. *The Elusive Presence*. San Francisco: Harper & Row, 1978.

Thompson, Leonard H. *Introducing Biblical Literature*. Englewood Cliffs: Prentice-Hall, 1978.

Tikkun. Vol. 1, No. 2, 1986.

Toombs, *The Old Testament in Christian Preaching*. Philadelphia: Westminster, 1961.

Vawter, Bruce. *A Path through Genesis*. New York: Sheed & Ward, 1956.

Von Rod, Gerhard. *God at Work in Israel.* Translated by John H. Marks. Nashville: Abingdon, 1981.

_____. *The Message of the Prophets.* Translated by D. M. G. Stalker. New York: Harper & Row, 1967.

Walter, Robert C., ed. *Bible Study Sourcebook: Old Testament.* Atlanta: John Knox Press, 1981.

Weber, Hans-Ruedi. *Experiments with Bible Study.* Philadelphia: Westminster, 1981.

Westermann, Claus. *A Thousand Years and a Day.* American ed. Philadelphia: Muhlenberg, 1962.

Williamson, H. G. M. *Word Biblical Commentary.* Vol. 16. Ezra, Nehemiah. Edited by David A. Hubbard, Glen W. Barker, John D. Watts and Ralph P. Martin. Waco: Word Books, 1985.

Wiesel, Elie. *Five Biblical Portraits: Saul, Jonah, Jeremiah, Elijah, Joshua.* Notre Dame: University of Notre Dame Press, 1981.

Wink, Walter. *The Bible in Human Trans-Formation.* Philadelphia: Fortress, 1973.

Wood, Leon. *Distressing Days of the Judges.* Grand Rapids: Zondervan, 1978.

Youngblood, Ronald. *Faith of Our Fathers.* Glendale: Regal Books, 1976.